Have Kid,
Will Travel

Have Kid, Will Travel

101 Survival Strategies for Vacationing with Babies and Young Children

Claire Tristram

**Andrews McMeel
Publishing**

Kansas City

Library of Congress Cataloging-in-Publication Data

Tristram, Claire.
    Have kid, will travel : 101 survival strategies for vacationing with babies and young children / Claire Tristram.
        p.   cm.
    ISBN 0-8362-2719-0 (pbk.)
    1. Parent and child. 2. Children—Travel. 3. Infants—Travel.
4. Family recreation. 5. Vacations—Planning. I. Title.
HQ755.85.T75 1997
306.874—dc21   96-48271
                                                       CIP

To Mom and Dad:

All of the love in this book came first from you.

Contents

Have Kid, Will Travel

Foreword

Every once in a while we find a book that we know at first glance is one we "need." This applied to me before I had finished the first chapter in *Have Kid, Will Travel*. I also knew that the "we" meant not only myself, now thinking as a grandparent, but any parent or grandparent. As a retired pediatrician, my first thought was what I would have given during thirty-seven years in practice to have had such a source of practical information with which to help countless young parents think positively and happily about traveling with their children.

Probably never before now has vacation time and travel with young families been so common. Certainly even more is expected in the coming years. Businesses and industry are increasingly aware of the value of vacation time for their employees, and insist on it being used as R&R to prevent burnout and maintain productivity and high morale. And we are a nation that travels. At the same time, society has an increasing concern about the strength of the family and the time spent enjoying each other while nurturing our children and learning together from new experiences.

What better time could one chose to have such a book as this appear on the scene, complementing all the other books on parenting. This practical, enjoyable-to-read, first-time-ever book tells us that we can have fun with our kids by traveling with them, and shows us how to make it fun, easy, safe, and something we should not miss.

There is much about Claire Tristram's book that is genuinely unique. Her obvious knowledge of basic parenting needs and skills, and of child behavior and development and children's needs, gives great credibility to what she has written. She has used her natural instincts together with exhaustive research to bring this information to print. Her style and down-to-earth language, sprinkled with humor, makes for very easy reading, reminding me of Erma Bombeck's natural, easy humor, while telling it just as it is.

Every page is filled with practical tips about traveling with young children. So much practical, valuable information is a rare commodity to find in one book. It is a source of accurate information, ranging from the simplest needs, such as caring for infants and young children, feeding and clothing them, and keeping them contented, occupied, and happy away from home, to important safety issues and educational opportunities, whether during an afternoon outing at the beach or a month-long trip to a dude ranch or foreign land.

A unique and valuable part of the book is the abundance of data on where and with whom to check for more information and specific items useful in traveling with young children. Included are names, addresses, and phone and FAX numbers. All is most useful for any parent. It takes the fear out of the experience you are planning and makes you feel like jumping in and giving it a try!

I feel certain that this book will be recommended by pediatricians to parents as the standard source of information on traveling with kids. Nowhere else is this comprehensive information available. The wise travel agent will be sure to make parents aware of this book, which encourages us to go vacationing with our children and grandchildren. It may be the best opportunity of our lives, and also of the children's.

Clearly *Have Kid, Will Travel* is a one-of-a-kind book for any parent to review and use when planning vacation travel with infants and small children. Read it for enjoyment, as a source of specific guidance, and to have fun with your children on every vacation or trip away from home.

H. JAMES HOLROYD, M.D., FAAP

Introduction

When I was four years old, my parents put me, my brother, my sister, and our family dog into the backseat of a car and took us all on a two-week road trip, the first real adventure of our lives. I learned what *big* meant from standing at the lip of the Grand Canyon and looking out over the biggest hole I'd ever seen. I learned what *lucky* was when my dad put a nickel into a slot machine in a Nevada drugstore and twenty-eight dollars spilled out, bouncing away in every direction on the linoleum floor. I learned what *empty* meant from watching tumbleweeds roll along a stretch of lonely highway on the Texas panhandle. Although I was only four, I have no doubt that this trip created in me a love of travel so deep that I've since lived in or visited fifty states and over thirty countries.

And when my own daughter, Lucille, was just six days old, I held her in my arms and took her for a walk along a beach. As we walked, she breathed deeply, as if tasting the air. She turned her face toward the setting sun and waved her arms in a way she never had before. Lucille doesn't specifically recall the experience, of course. But I have no doubt that the newborn I held in my arms that day was enjoying our walk, and that her experience will shape the way she relates to the world as she grows up.

The first five years are the most magical time to vacation with your children. It's a time when they are changing more rapidly than at any other time of their lives. They are learning from you every day. What you show them about the world now will change their lives in profound ways.

The first five years can also be the most challenging time to vacation with your children. Maybe you've experienced those evenings at restaurants where everything landed on the floor when your child pulled the tablecloth. Or you needed to cut your beach vacation short last year when your child tried to eat the beach. If you're a parent, you know from your own daily experience how much attention your children require.

During the course of my research for this book, I've asked hundreds of parents to share with me their secrets for happy, relaxing vacations with children five and under. Here, in order, are the answers I heard most often:

Leave them at home.
Wait until they're older.
Have good kids.

The sad thing is, these parents weren't joking. For most of us, leisure time is precious. With maybe ten days off a year plus a smattering of national holidays, we're often afraid to risk big trips with our very young children. What if we squander our two weeks on a family vacation that leaves us so exhausted that we need another two weeks to recover? What if our kids don't behave? What if it's just too hard?

Maybe the most common fear is that our children are too young to enjoy the vacation we plan, anyway. We all want to be good parents: We might feel that it's unwise, or even cruel, to subject our children to the rigors of traveling to a new place. If you've had these kinds of thoughts, then it is for you, especially, that I've written this book.

I believe that with a little planning, and armed with the right information, you can have a vacation with your young children that renews and refreshes you, and that gives your children the kinds of memories and experiences that will last a lifetime. No matter how young they are. Unlike any other guide book, this book isn't about where to go with your kids, but how.

A word about language: Where possible, I've written "children" instead of "child," both to avoid the problem of whether to call your child a "he" or a "she," and to make those of you with just one child all the more grateful that you don't need to manage more on your trip. When it's been necessary to write in the singular, I've used "she."

Enjoy your trip! And when you come back, feel free to share with me any comments and suggestions you might have. You can write to me in care of my publisher, or you can reach me via the Internet at claire@tristram.com.

Chapter 1
Planning Is More Than What to Pack

By and large, mothers and housewives are the only workers who do not have regular time off. They are the great vacationless class.—Anne Morrow Lindbergh

This chapter is primarily for you. Not your kids. They come later. For a moment, take a break from worrying about how you will keep them safe and happy during your upcoming vacation. For a moment, think of yourself. As a parent with young children, you need a vacation almost by definition. It comes with the territory.

Maybe you and your spouse both work sixty-hour weeks and you only have ten days' vacation this year. Or you're a single parent, looking forward to finally having some quality time with your children. Or maybe you're a stay-at-home parent, looking forward to letting your spouse help take care of the kids so you'll finally have time to relax. Whatever your situation is, if you're a parent with young children, your leisure time is precious. Here's how to make the most of your time.

1. Five secrets for stress-free vacations with your kids
Here they are:

1. **Ask yourself, "Where do *I* want to go on this vacation?" Then *go*.**

   Small children don't need to be an anchor around your neck. Instead of asking yourself, "Where can I still go on vacation, now that I have children?" begin with the belief that you can go anywhere you want, and that your children will enjoy the same kinds of experiences that you find enjoyable.

2. **Travel *with* your kids, not *for* your kids.**

   No matter how young, your children are your travel partners. They shouldn't be the central focus of the trip, but they also shouldn't be tag-alongs without any say in your itinerary.

   Involve your children as much as possible in the logistics of your trip. If they're too young to talk, you'll need to be their proxy when you make your travel plans, and to represent their wishes in the choices you make. Involve your older children by sharing maps, videos, and picture books with them before you go. Even an eighteen-month-old will begin to understand and anticipate the trip, and may even have suggestions of her own.

3. **Expect to lose spontaneity, but to gain all the more in surprises.**

   You can't be as spontaneous as you were before your children were born. That's a fact. But don't think that will make your vacations dull and predictable. Your perspective will be changed in ways you don't expect. Even vacation destinations that you've returned to year after year will be completely new and fresh when you bring your children along. And don't be dismayed when things sometimes go awry. Expect them to! Even vacations without children are rarely glitch-free.

4. **Know what to expect.**

   Before you leave, take time to make a realistic assessment of how many hours a day you spend caring for your children. Think of a typical day when you're not working outside the home, and when you are completely responsible for their care. How many hours are you engaged in activities that feel to you like "work"? That might include cooking, feeding the kids, dressing them, picking up after them, running errands, getting them settled into bed. These things won't go away magically when you're on vacation. The better you appreciate them, the more chance you have of not letting them overwhelm you.

5. Get the help you need to have a good time.

If your realistic assessment of the "work" required to take care of your children threatens to overwhelm your time for play, then do something about it. It can be as simple as asking a spouse for more help, or as elaborate as choosing a resort that offers child care. This book is full of helpful strategies for reducing the work, so you have more time to enjoy your children's company.

2. Planning tips for couples

Good family vacations mean that everyone will feel refreshed and relaxed when it's over. Unlike your carefree preparent days, however, it's going to require planning, especially if one spouse normally takes a much greater role than the other in taking care of the children. When you go on vacation, all of the work of parenting your children comes along with you.

Take time to sit down with your spouse and to discuss how you'll help one another have a wonderful trip. Here are some questions to get you started:

1. How much of the time do we want to be with our children, how much with each other, and how much alone to pursue our own interests?

Most couples welcome the time to be with their children, but also realize that time away from them can be just as important. Be honest about your needs, so you can plan a vacation that fulfills them.

2. How will we divide parenting responsibilities while on vacation?

Your children will still need you to change their diapers, feed them, calm their fears, and keep them safe, even though you're on vacation. And sometimes your children will be fussy and tired and in need of some extra love.

Try to divide the responsibilities for caring for your children so that you're both doing the things you enjoy most with them, anyway. Or agree that your spouse will take primary care of your children each morning, and that you will take on that task in the afternoon. Be realistic about the amount of time it will take to be with your children and to take care of their basic needs.

It's hard to overestimate how important a discussion like this one is for happy vacations. It's the most important planning you'll do. Make time for it. Otherwise it's quite likely that you'll waste precious vacation time arguing about how the other spouse isn't doing enough to help out.

3. Planning tips for single parents

As a single parent, the most difficult challenge for you on vacation will be to avoid getting overwhelmed by your children's needs, and to find time for your own.

If you have only one child, your vacation planning can actually be easier than if you were traveling with a spouse. There won't be any potential misunderstandings about who is responsible for taking care of your child's needs. Without even thinking about it, you'll slow your schedule down in response to your child.

But when your children begin to outnumber you, you'll need to plan ahead to make sure you still have a good time. Here are some questions to ask yourself before you go:

1. How much of my vacation time do I want to spend with my children?

Your initial reaction might be "100 percent, of course!" And it might be the right answer. But allow yourself the luxury of planning for a little time away from them, too, if that's what you need to feel like you've had a vacation.

2. **How can I make the "work" part of my vacation easier so I have time to enjoy myself?**

If you're on your own, these responsibilities can soak up all of your vacation time, leaving you feeling like you never left home. Plan ahead for that contingency. Plan for the kind of help you need to make your vacation fun. It may be as simple as staying with friends or relatives, or as elaborate as choosing a full-service resort that has baby-sitting services on call when you need them. You may decide to travel with a friend who has children the same age as yours, or with a group. Don't underestimate the work of parenting your children, and end up feeling like you never left home.

4. **Ten vacation destinations to avoid with babies and young children**

In general, you'll have no trouble thinking of vacations to avoid—you'll be so busy worrying about why you shouldn't go on the vacation you want, now that you have children, that you'll rule out some very do-able trips. In only a handful of circumstances will you be right, that the effort to take your children along will be too great for you to have a good time. A cross-country motorcycle trip, for example. Or any of the below circumstances, all of which will be more enjoyable when they're older:

1. **Theme parks.** They're expensive, always crowded, and may even frighten your children at this age. Every hotel within forty miles of the park will be overpriced. In a few years, your kids will have forgotten you've taken them there and will be pestering you to go again. Wait until they're older.
2. **Most "family" resorts.** With rare exceptions, which should be championed for their dedication to families with small children, the places that bill themselves as

"family" resorts are designed with older kids in mind. You'll end up staying at a place that neither you nor your kids enjoy, and paying for a lot of services you don't use.

3. **Any tour that requires you to sign an indemnity clause.** "Adventure" travel—whether it's rafting down the Colorado or trekking through the Himalayas—is in vogue right now, even for families with very small children. Many trips are well-run and safe, but some are not. If you're asked to sign a form releasing the tour operator from liability if your kids are harmed, what does that say about the tour group's faith in their trip's safety? Better to skip it.

4. **Tacky tourist attractions.** Especially if you've already seen them yourself. Like theme parks, they're best when your kids have reached at least elementary-school age.

5. **Any show that has expensive tickets.** A ride in a grocery store cart will offer as much or more fun for young children as any "Barney on Ice" show can. Save the family shows for a few more years.

6. **Advance-purchase tickets.** It's best to be as free and as flexible with your plans as possible when you're taking the kids. Whenever possible, avoid getting tied down to being in a certain place at a certain time several months in the future.

7. **Art exhibits.** Especially if they're big events, since they'll be crowded and your child won't be able to see anything. You usually won't be able to take either a stroller or a backpack-style carrier into museums, either. If you decide to go anyway, try to pick a weekday morning, when the crowds are less likely, and don't count on staying much longer than half an hour.

8. **Any event in an indoor arena.** Planning to take in a pro hockey game, basketball game, or other indoor event? Try it in the cheap seats, if at all. Or splurge for

a private booth, if you're a real fan. You'll be amazed at how loud, and how frightening, the public address system will sound to your baby, to say nothing of a crowd of roaring fans. Older kids may take the noise in stride, but will soon be bored and won't like being confined to such a narrow seat.

9. **Anywhere without shade.** Beaches are fine, as long as the beach rules allow you to bring an umbrella, canopy, or better yet a tent to protect your child from the heat and sun. But avoid going places where you won't be able to protect your child—like outdoor concerts or sporting events, where an umbrella will block the view of the people behind you.

10. **Anywhere you don't feel comfortable bringing your children along.** Children are adaptable, wonderful travel companions. But if you are worried about their safety, or concerned that their presence will be annoying to others, then you'll be too tense to enjoy yourself.

5. Getting your kids ready for the big trip

For about a week before your planned departure, play it extra safe with your children's health. After you've been outside the house or interacting with other people, wash your hands before touching your children, and don't allow anyone else to touch them without washing first, since colds are usually passed from direct physical contact. If your children are enrolled in day care, ask the caregivers to be especially diligent about keeping toys away from them that have been handled or mouthed by other children, particularly the ones with runny noses.

Take along anything that will help your child cope with a radically new environment, whether it be a familiar stuffed toy, an old blanket, or another familiar object. But don't overdo it: The most comforting "object" of all will be you, and most children will adapt readily to a new environment if they know a parent is there to keep them safe. Light packing means less stuff to worry about carrying along or losing when you get there. It's particularly important to travel light when going by any mode of transportation besides your car, since you'll need to keep track of your children as well as your luggage. Wherever you're going, people there are likely to have babies of their own, and hence baby supplies.

Even if you think your children are too young to understand what you say, take a little time before you go to explain the trip you're planning, how long you'll be gone, and what they can expect to see while you're away. Your children might understand more than you think they do, and acknowledging their participation in the family trip is a good habit to get into, since one day they'll know as much as you do. Maybe even a little more.

6. Before you go: a checklist

Now that you've spent time thinking about the important stuff—how to have fun, how to make sure your family has fun, and how to make sure your vacation is all you want it to be—you can move on to the more mundane tasks of getting out the door. Here's a list to help you:

1. Stop mail and newspaper delivery. Better yet, avoid any overt sign that you'll be gone by getting a house sitter.
2. If you don't use a house sitter, be sure to ask a neighbor to watch for any parcels or other hand-delivered goods while you're gone. Arrange to have your lawn mowed, too, to avoid having your house look abandoned.
3. Leave an itinerary of where you will be, and when, with your neighbor in case there's a problem and you need to be reached.
4. Empty your refrigerator of anything that will spoil while you're away, and ask your neighbor to take out the garbage for you on trash day. Wash all the dishes and put them away, and run your garbage disposal a long time to clear it completely.
5. Turn off unnecessary utilities. Adjust your thermostat. Unplug appliances, especially if you live in an area with electrical storms. Put lights on timers to simulate your regular patterns of daily living.

6. Before you go out the door, check to see that every door and window is locked.

7. As you leave, take the time to look at your beautiful family and say to yourself, *my children make wonderful travel companions.* Take time to feel how true it is. Your children love you, trust you, and are just waiting for you to show them the world. Let go of what everyone else thinks—that vacationing with children is difficult, unpleasant, and complicated. It isn't. It's magical. It's learning how to be a family. It's the adventure of your lifetime. The more you believe it, the better it will become.

Chapter 2
First Trips

I never knew anyone could be so small.—a new father

Learning to travel with your baby takes practice, especially if it's your first. How soon you go out, and how far, will depend not only on how your baby feels, but also on how you feel. Here are some guidelines for enjoying your first trips together.

7. When is it safe to travel with my newborn?

The short answer to this question is: When you're ready. Chances are your infant is more ready for a trip than you are. New mothers need time to recover, no matter how uncomplicated their labor and delivery. New fathers need time to adjust to the reality of being awakened every two or three hours by the new family member. And other children in the family need to be reassured that they are still loved. None of you may feel like taking a trip just yet.

Once your baby is given a clean bill of health from your doctor, though, then she's ready to go out, as long as the temperature outside is above freezing and below 80 degrees. Don't overdress your baby, thinking she needs extra warmth: A single extra layer from what makes you comfortable is just about right. Sun exposure should be kept to a minimum, though, by keeping your baby in the shade and dressing her in long-sleeved clothing and a hat.

A lot of parents worry needlessly about the fragility of their newborn, and about exposing their newborn to germs. If you don't allow strangers to handle your baby, and you keep her away from friends and family members who are sick, then you need not be overly concerned with taking her out.

Obviously you'll want to avoid travel to any area where there is incidence of a disease that your child can't receive the recommended immunizations or prescribed treatment for because she is too young. Beyond that, it's up to you.

8. What newborns experience

As soon as she is born, your child can distinguish light from dark, rough from smooth, her mother's voice from other voices. What's more, she is able to express preferences, form opinions, and create memories from her experiences. The richer those experiences are, the richer the mental landscape of your baby will be.

Your baby is born with her sense of touch, taste, and smell more or less fully developed. Development of her hearing and sight, however, depends greatly on her getting enough practice using them during the first two years of life. When you expose your baby to interesting sights and sounds, you are actually helping to create permanent neural connections in her brain that are critical for her development.

Take your newborn out into the world with you. Watch how she notices a new sound, an unfamiliar object, or an unexpected smell carried on the breeze. Everything in the world is new and fresh and wonderful to your baby. Let her teach you. By being with your newborn, and observing her reactions to her experiences, you will notice once again the things you've grown accustomed to, and you'll rediscover for yourself the sensual richness of the world.

9. First trips with your newborn

Parents have taken their newborns with them on photo safaris in Kenya, on backpacking trips in Alaska, to the Super Bowl, or anywhere else in between that you can think of.

But most of us just aren't that organized or that daring. We're amazed at how fragile the baby looks, even if we have other children. And we're so overwhelmed by the new arrival that we're still trying to figure out how to find time to get ourselves into the shower, much less out the door.

It's worth the effort to make a habit of going out with your baby, no matter how overwhelming the prospect might seem in the beginning. It will refresh both you and her. Some good first trips for mortal parents include these:

1. **A walk.** It sounds simple, but isn't. You need to get yourself ready, dress your baby, figure out how to get your baby into her stroller or baby carrier, and schedule your walk so you're leaving when she's fed and rested. You may also have an active toddler or other children to get ready at the same time. It's complicated, but worth it: A walk can be a tremendously rejuvenating experience. Many times a fussy baby will calm right down in the fresh air. And it's great practice for more ambitious journeys.

2. **A trip to the mall.** Not to shop—that's an art in itself when you have children along, and not at all relaxing. But indoor malls are great places to watch more experienced moms handle their brood, especially if yours is a winter baby and it's too cold outside for her. Malls also have a level of anonymity that makes them good places for practicing public nursing. Pick a bench, sit down with your baby, and watch the passing parade.

3. **A visit to friends or family.** You'll get the incredible lift of having the people you love tell you how beautiful your baby is, and how lucky you are—always good reminders after a few days of nonstop nursing, or of sleeping less than three hours a night. And you'll have help with the baby when you get there, maybe even the chance to take a well-deserved nap while adoring fans hold your little one in their laps.

10. Vacations with your newborn

The first several weeks after a new baby is born is often the longest time that mothers can afford to be away from their workplace, and it can also be a very easy time for fathers to ask for and get vacation time. Here are some ways to make a vacation with your newborn a great experience for both child and parent:

1. Since you can't be sure when your baby is going to arrive, or how you'll feel when she gets here, make your vacation plans for at least a month after your due date, and make them as flexible and easy to cancel as possible. Most women will need about a month before they feel recovered from even the smoothest labor and delivery.
2. Talk with your doctor or midwife before you make your plans, so that you can make appropriate choices about how far you want to travel from their care, and what contingency medical services you'll want to have on call at your destination.
3. Choose a destination that pampers you, where your needs are taken care of so that you have all the time in the world to be with your new baby.

11. What to bring

Even for a half-hour trip to the supermarket, new parents like to take along the diaper bag stuffed full with a dozen diapers, a box of baby wipes, six receiving blankets, three changes of clothing, a changing pad, two tubes of ointment, a bottle of baby oil, and a pacifier or two.

Not necessary. Here is the rule: Bring the least amount of paraphernalia that you possibly can. For some parents, that will be one or two diapers, plus a handful of wipes stowed in a sandwich bag in their purse or back pocket. A plastic grocery bag can be your "waterproof changing pad" and can hold the dirty diaper when you're through. It may take a month or two to get used to the minimalist approach, but the less you lug along, the easier you'll find getting around with your new baby, and the more likely you are to make a habit of going out.

What about extended vacations? Keeping the minimalist rule firmly in mind, take what you need to feel comfortable and confident that you'll be able to take care of your baby as easily as if you were at home. Here's a list to get you thinking:

Must-haves:

1. **One diaper for each hour of travel time, plus a supply to last until you plan to shop for more.**
2. **Two vinyl diaper wraps with Velcro closures.** (Even if you use disposable diapers, diaper wraps take very little space in your bag and are useful insurance against leaks.)
3. **Three receiving blankets.** Why three? One for laying your baby down on, one to cover her, and one to use over your shoulder to protect your clothes while burping her.
4. **Seasonally appropriate clothes.** One to two outfits per day, for up to a week or so, at which time you'll probably want to wash them anyway. Long-sleeved cotton suits that are open at the bottom, instead of having legs, are best for travel, since they give you easy access to her diaper.
5. **Plastic grocery bags (for soiled clothes and diapers).**
6. **Diaper rash ointment.**
7. **Premoistened wipes.**
8. **A sling or child carrier designed for newborns.** These are lighter and easier to pack than a stroller. They're also better for your baby, and better for you. A 1986 study at the McGill University–Montreal Children's Hospital Research Institute of ninety-nine babies three to twelve weeks old showed that babies who were picked up and held in their parents' arms or a carrier for at least three hours a day cried 43 percent less overall and 51 percent less during the evening hours than those who weren't picked up until they began to cry. Less crying means a more relaxing vacation time for you.

9. **A lightweight, collapsible bassinet (if necessary).**
   Or the baby can sleep with you.
10. **An infant safety seat for automobile travel.**

12. Five reasons not to wait until she's older

1. The more easy confidence you develop now in taking
   your newborn with you, the easier it will be to have fun
   with her on vacations and longer trips. Practice the
   basics of getting around with her as early and often as
   possible so you don't have to sweat the small stuff on
   your big trips.
2. Just how long are you going to wait? Some parents
   don't go on a vacation with their kids until they are out
   of diapers—but what if you have another baby in the
   meantime?
3. Your newborn's brain is literally forming as you read
   this. The breadth of experience she has at a young age
   will influence her relationship with the world, and
   even her success within it. Don't make the mistake of
   thinking she's too young to gain from the experience of
   going out with you—every moment, she's learning in
   ways you can't even imagine.
4. For many mothers with careers outside the home, the
   six weeks after the baby is born is the longest uninterrupted time they will ever have with their child. For
   many fathers, it's an easy time to ask their employers for
   vacation time. Why not spend some of those early days
   with your baby on vacation, in a comfortable environment where your cleaning and cooking are taken care of
   and you can spend all of your time adoring your baby?
5. Frequent, short trips with your newborn now will get
   you into the habit of being a family that spends time and
   has fun together. Too many parents feel tied down by
   their young infants, and may even begin to resent the
   loss of freedom. Don't feel that way. The more you and
   your baby become accustomed to traveling together,
   the more you'll both get out of the experience.

Chapter 3
Vacation Planning as Your Children Grow

*Every stage of development is complete in itself.
The three year old is not an incomplete five year
old. The child is not an incomplete adult. Never are
we simply on our way! Always we have arrived!
Enjoy now!*

—J.C. Pearce

Suppose you're thinking of going on a big trip. But you worry whether your children are too young to enjoy it. You may have doubts about dragging them along when they have no choice in the matter. You may even have had a few twinges of feeling incredibly selfish—how could you put your children through such an ordeal?

Think again. If you're taking care of their health as well as their need to be nurtured by you, they will benefit from traveling along with you. Don't make the mistake of judging what they will experience by your own standards: Your children will have their own way of learning and enjoying what you show them.

Let's take an example. Suppose you take a trip to Spain that includes a visit to the Alhambra on a late summer afternoon.

Your experience will be from an adult's perspective. Maybe you resonate with its history, or stop to appreciate the mathematical precision of its architecture.

Your three-month-old child won't care about those things, of course, yet she enjoys the place you've brought her, in her own way. She grows quiet in your arms as you walk about, fascinated by the contrast between the bright sunshine of the gardens and the cool shade under the arches.

What if your child is an eighteen-month-old? She may discover, to her delight, that her high-pitched cries will echo back to her in marvelous ways through the arches. A three-year-old will want to climb into the fountains. A five-year-old will ply you with questions about who built the Alhambra, and where they are now.

The point is, all of the members of your family can have valid and positive experiences, as long as you provide your children with a loving and safe environment when you travel, an environment that respects their level of development. You will learn from your children, too, as they show you things about a place that you never would have noticed without their company.

13. Vacations with your three- to eight-month-old baby

When your baby reaches three months, her colic, if she had it, is over its worst stages. She may begin to sleep through the night, or at least wake up less often. She's marvelously portable, still almost as easy to carry as a newborn, yet requiring less fuss, fewer diaper changes, and fewer feedings. You yourself are rested, comfortable, and confident. Take advantage of this time! Parents of toddlers look back fondly on the time when they could still put their child down and know that she'd stay (relatively) put—after eight months of age or so vacations definitely become more challenging. Planning a vacation for when your new baby will be three to eight months old is also a great way to get through those last few months of pregnancy.

Where you go really depends on you, since your baby will be happy to be with you, wherever you go. Do choose a place that makes you feel welcome, however. That probably means choosing a hotel that doesn't have thin walls, or where you have a separate unit to yourself. Also choose to stay at a place with a kitchen. Your child will be more wakeful than a newborn, so it will be more difficult to time restaurant meals around naps, and she'll still be too young to understand why she should be quiet when you take her out to dinner. In fact, she's likely to be testing the volume control on her vocal cords during this age, making the option of staying home for meals a very attractive one.

What should you bring? Take a look at the list for newborns on pages 20 and 21; add a couple of washable bibs, a baby spoon, and a stroller. Take a portable breast pump if you are breast-feeding, to give you time away from your baby if you want it. Keep it simple. Stick with cotton clothes that are easy to wash by hand.

Take your baby along with you on day trips or weekends before the big vacation comes. These trips will give you an opportunity to get to know your baby's rhythms, her likes and dislikes, and her tolerance for new environments. That tolerance will build as she travels more with you—remember that we humans are by nature nomadic.

Respect your baby's needs while on vacation, and make time for them. Choose a vacation where it won't be a chore to diaper her every hour and feed her every three hours. Some parents will be organized enough to fit that right into a bicycle tour through China. For the rest of us, though, a nice, lazy beach vacation will be just about right with a child this age. If you do choose to vacation at a sunny locale, be sure to bring along a baby-size tent, a covered, portable playpen, or to find another shaded area for your baby to sleep and play away from the sun's rays, since sunscreen usually isn't recommended for infants until they are at least six months old. There are many options to choose from, available at retail stores.

After being a new parent for a few months, you're likely to need a break, some time away from your child. (Time at your workplace doesn't count as time off.) Make sure to build in some free time when you're responsible to no one but yourself by choosing a vacation destination where you can arrange for responsible child care when you need it.

14. Vacations with your eight-month- to three-year-old child

The path from eight months to three years is a huge developmental journey, as any parent will tell you. But for parents planning a vacation with children between these ages, this period of your child's life will have similar challenges, from beginning to end.

From eight months to three years, your child is old enough to move around independently, but too young to stay out of trouble when she does. She is old enough to be bored and too young to consistently entertain herself. She's old enough to know she's in an unfamiliar place but too young to really understand what's going on. She's old enough to like daily routines and too young to understand why those routines sometimes need to change. Top it all off with feeding and dressing a child who can't do either herself yet, plus potty training that still isn't 100 percent foolproof, and you have a real challenge on your hands.

Does that mean you stay home for two years? Of course not. This is one of the best times to be with your children. This time encompasses everything from your child's first word to her first steps. And it's the time when you, as a parent, are all the more likely to need a vacation.

Destination planning is critical with children this age. Choose a place where you don't have to constantly be saying no-no-no to your child as you pull her away from danger. Really pay attention to where you choose to stay. Be meticulous about asking potential hotels about their willingness to cooperate with childproofing your room. Take time to find a place that offers safe, enclosed play areas on-site or nearby. Choose a destination where you'll be able to let your child run around freely for at least part of the day, without running into traffic, poison oak, or worse.

Even if you haven't previously considered using an outfitter, resort operator, or packaged tour for your family vacation, now is a good time to reconsider, especially for more ambitious plans such as an outdoor camping and hiking expedition or a bike tour. If the thought of vacationing with your active toddler while still trying to enjoy a real vacation yourself seems an impossible task, investigate these packaged options with a good family travel agent. She should be able to suggest alternatives that either give you a little time away from your child to catch your breath, or that take care of all the other details that go into good vacation planning, so that you can feel free and easy to spend quality time with your family.

From about eight months on, your child may begin to suffer acute separation anxiety and stranger anxiety. She may be very unhappy about being away from you, particularly in an unfamiliar environment. Take it slow if you plan to use a baby-sitter or child-care facility while on vacation. Wait a couple of days until your child has gotten used to a place, and limit your time away, at least at first, to only a couple of hours a day. Although stranger anxiety and separation anxiety are normal, that doesn't make them any easier for your child.

Having fun while vacationing with your toddler requires you to plan your day, especially if you aren't using the help of a baby-sitter for any part of that day. Here are three rules to keep in mind to make the vacation enjoyable and relaxing for everyone in your family:

1. Schedule running-around time faithfully each day of your vacation, so that your child can enjoy and release her abundant energy. Make it part of your itinerary for at least an hour a day—whether you're letting her run around in an empty conference room on the mezzanine level of your city hotel, or enjoying a morning together in the upper meadows at Tuolumne in Yosemite National Park, or simply taking a break in a municipal playground near your destination that offers plenty of free space.

2. Depending on your child, the difference between a great vacation day and an impossible, what-am-I-doing-here

experience all comes down to one question: Did she have her nap? Plan accordingly, and plan for every day. Will she sleep in her stroller or child carrier? Then you have it made. Bring her stroller along if you're going to be out during nap time. If that doesn't work for her, though, choose a vacation destination where an in-room siesta will be a pleasant experience for you both, and where that room is located right where you want to be, anyway. It's a good time to splurge for the beachfront room, instead of economizing on the hotel three blocks away.

3. Be respectful of bedtime routines that your child has come to love and depend on. Make time for them. Obviously if you're camping or in an otherwise very different environment you'll have to improvise. But a little attention at bedtime makes for a peaceful night and a happy child.

The more you give in to and make time for these rules, the less like work they become. Instead, you'll be sharing a wonderful experience. It's okay to need time to yourself or with your spouse while on vacation, too, of course. Just make sure that your child's day still includes free time to play, nap time, a bedtime routine, and that your child's caregiver understands what is required.

15. Vacations with your three- to five-year-old child

Sometime between your child's third and sixth birthday, she'll experience the first vacation that she'll consciously remember when she's older. That makes vacations with children this age a very important time.

Make her a partner in your vacation planning. Really spend time with her, explaining where you're going, how you'll get there, and what you'll see. Ask her what she thinks, and give her an opportunity to voice her opinions. Show her pictures and read guidebooks to her, and let her pick a special place for you to go together, once you're there.

When on vacation, look for opportunities to introduce your child to other children her own age. Being with and playing with other children is very important at this age, and it will make for some wonderful memories. Give your child space and time to play with her new companions.

If you also have other, younger children, it's tremendously important not to let the baby of the family consume all of your energy. Schedule time with your older child alone, every day if you can, even if it's for just a half-hour. Once a week or so, schedule something really special, like Dad's night out just with his daughter, or Mom spending an afternoon at a municipal playground with just her son along. Take time for *this* child, and to make your child feel special and loved.

If there's one rule that every parent should follow, without fail, with three- to five-year-old children, it's this: Follow through on your promises. If you don't, your child will remind you of your failure every day of your vacation, and may even bring it up decades later.

16. The art of low-maintenance dressing
You can spend a lifetime dressing them, feeding them, putting them to sleep—but the fact is, when you're on vacation, you won't want to. What follows are some suggestions of how to streamline the more time-consuming elements of being a parent, so vacations will *feel* like vacations. Not all of these suggestions will work for every parent, but at the very least, you'll know how much time you're taking on a given activity every day, and begin to formulate time-saving strategies of your own. Let's start with low-maintenance dressing.

FOR INFANTS:

Use disposable diapers. No pins, no covers, no fuss. They also absorb up to one quart of liquid, which makes many parents comfortable with fewer diaper changes.
Time saved: thirty minutes a day.

Use flushable diaper liners. Technically, you're supposed to be rinsing your baby's messy disposables out in the

toilet before throwing them away. By using flushable diaper liners you'll be fulfilling that obligation, and you'll have less mess to figure out how to dispose of.
Time saved: ten minutes a day, or at the very least you'll get rid of the guilt of not doing it.

Dress her in sack suits with open bottoms, no legs, and long sleeves. You'll get protection from the sun and will have easy access to her bottom for a much quicker change. Buy two to five sack suits, all the same, in a cotton blend that you can wash in the sink.
Time saved: it depends on how dexterous you were with those snaps you'll no longer have to snap; roughly ten minutes a day.

Skip the booties. They fall off, anyway. And toes are cute. Dress her in sack suits that cover her feet instead.
Time saved: variable, but significant.

Buy some drool bibs if she spits up often. You'll save time by not needing to change her clothes so often, and will prolong time between needing to do laundry.
Time saved: ten minutes a day.

FOR OLDER CHILDREN:

Buy five vacation "uniforms." Choose a clothing style that will work for the duration of the trip, and buy two to five identical sets of it, depending on how dirty your child likes to get. No choice means no looking around for what goes with what, and no arguing with your child about what to wear today.
Time saved: ten to thirty minutes a day.

Sew it on. If traveling to a cold climate, sew mittens and hats onto your child's outer jacket.
Time saved looking for lost mittens: five minutes a day.

Go Velcro. If traveling to a warm climate, choose Velcro-secured, rubber-soled sandals for your children's feet. They can get wet, your children don't need socks, and they give their feet nearly as much support as a sneaker.
Time saved: five minutes a day.

17. The art of nutritious, low-maintenance meals

Meals can be a real time-sink. Here are some ways to keep that from happening.

FOR EVERYONE:

Rent a room with a kitchen. Don't plan to go out for more than one meal a day, and make the other meals simple, picnic-style affairs.
Time saved: easily one hour a day.

FOR INFANTS:

Breast-feed. Obviously there are more important reasons to breast-feed your baby than your vacation plans, but it's still worth mentioning. You save the time you'd spend buying and preparing formula. If you're planning a big trip, you can even delay weaning to take advantage of breast-feeding's speed, good nutrition, and relative efficiency when compared with a tot trying to spoon-feed herself. Until your children are a year old or so (check with your pediatrician) you can also reintroduce breast-feeding while on a big trip, at mealtimes when you've started to feed your baby solid food, with no deleterious effects.
Time saved: ten to thirty minutes a day.

Buy premixed formula and disposable bottles. If you are bottle-feeding your child, make it as easy as possible on yourself by buying products that travel well. Premixed formula and disposable bottles let you avoid the mess of mixing and cleaning up afterward.
Time saved: thirty minutes a day.

Don't sterilize bottles. If your baby is bottle-fed, don't worry about boiling all your supplies. Most pediatricians now say it isn't necessary in areas where you don't need to worry about the safety of the water. (Where tap water isn't safe to drink, obviously, you'll need to boil the heck out of everything.)
Time saved: five minutes a day.

Don't heat formula. Heresy, you say? Some pediatricians think that feeding a baby formula that's at room temperature actually prevents stomach upsets! In any case, there's no medical reason to heat your baby's formula, and you'll avoid a potential burning hazard, especially if you're trying to heat it in an unfamiliar microwave oven. You also won't have to figure out a way to warm it up when you're on the road.
Time saved: forty minutes a day for a fully bottle-fed baby.

FOR OLDER CHILDREN:

Forget strained stuff. Don't travel when your baby is six to nine months old—when you're starting to introduce the concept of food, but can't feed herself yet. At nine months, she can begin to pick up her food. Good, non-messy finger foods include: tiny, well-steamed broccoli tips, well-cooked carrot cubes, ripe pears, banana bits, extra-firm tofu, and whole-wheat toast. By sticking with finger foods, you'll be able to eat your own meal at the same time. You'll also save the time it takes to spoon-feed her, and the time you'd normally have spent cleaning up gooey things from her hair and clothes—not to mention your own hair and clothes.
Time saved: twenty to forty minutes a day.

Plan menus and mealtimes. Stick with a schedule. Try to make breakfasts simple, lunches a picnic meal, and dinners uncomplicated.
Time saved: twenty minutes a day.

Don't fight with your children who are old enough to have developed food preferences. Let them decide what to eat while on vacation, within reason. Don't make an issue of the peas left on the plate, if it's holding up progress. Don't throw nutrition out the window, of course, but consciously try to choose foods on vacation that your children will like, rather than making mealtime a lesson in good eating habits.

Time saved: ten minutes a day.

18. Low-maintenance sleeping tips

Bedtime can be a time-consuming, even grim ordeal when on vacation. Your children may be uncomfortable in the new environment, or too wound up from the day's events to settle down. Here are some ways to make bedtime take *less* time:

Have a family bedtime. Go to bed at the same time as your children, a time halfway between your normal time to go to sleep and theirs. This strategy does away with the problem of sharing a room and expecting your children to go to sleep with the lights and the television on. It's a radical strategy, perhaps to be saved for times when you really need it, but definitely a good way to settle extremely wired children down.

Time saved: variable, but significant.

Let your children sleep with you. The idea of cosleeping is becoming more widely accepted in parenting books. Even if it's not your normal style, it has advantages for vacation time. Your children will feel supported in their new environment, and they will tend to settle down quickly and to feel safe if they wake up at night with you sleeping next to them.

Time saved: variable, but you could easily save an hour a night of needing to comfort a child to sleep who isn't happy with the unfamiliar surroundings.

Bring your own portable crib/playpen. If cosleeping doesn't work for your family, then bring your children's beds along with you. Even if the surroundings change, a child will get comfort from being in a familiar bed, and may have an easier time adjusting. This strategy is especially good for road trips—you won't need to look around for a place that provides a crib.

Time saved: variable, but you'll possibly be able to avoid an hour or so of settling-down tactics every night.

19. Other ways to eliminate time-wasters

If these work for you, great. If not, do spend some time looking for ways to become more efficient about the daily maintenance of your children. It will give you all the more time to enjoy them.

Skip the daily bath. Once every few days is more than enough, especially if they're in a pool all day.

Time saved: twenty minutes a day.

Give them haircuts. Long-haired children on trips equal tangles and tears. Short hair eliminates the problem and takes less time to care for every day.

Time saved: ten minutes a day.

Lighten up on life's lessons. Yes, your children will need to learn one day not to throw their shoes off the balcony. But try to keep the lessons you teach a little on the light side when you're on vacation, and to move on. You'll have time to reinforce those lessons later, when you're at home again. Your children are likely to be wound up and excitable, and not always on their best behavior; expect some mistakes. Save "time out" and other disciplinary measures for truly grave (i.e., life-threatening) situations.

Time saved: variable.

Enforce a no-TV rule. Better yet, stay somewhere without a television, or ask to have it removed from your room.

Time saved: if you're an average American family, three hours a day.

20. Finding the right travel agent

Travel agents who really cater to families—as opposed to those who put a few Disney tours in their portfolio—are few and far between. Even the good agents will usually focus on tours and trips for families with older children, not children under six, and certainly not children under two. Why? Because servicing families with very young children is *hard*. Anyone can suggest destinations that will be fun for an eight- to ten-year-old, or find the best airfares to a given city. But answering the questions that you'll have as a parent with young children, like: Which hotels have childproof rooms? Which tours provide baby-sitters on call? That's time-consuming, and requires an agent to really specialize in the young family market.

If you find an agent who is willing to invest the time, though, then you are well served by developing a relationship with her: Working through an agent will cost you nothing and may save you the time of doing the research yourself. Good agents will want to develop a long-standing relationship with you, and will demonstrate their desire to work with you by staying on top of airfare changes and by having firsthand knowledge of the places they suggest.

Here are some questions to ask your potential travel agent:

1. **How old are your children?** If your agent is raising a family, she's more likely to understand what your needs are. Your best bet will be to find an agent with children the same ages as your children—the agent will have the same needs as you do, and will be able to serve you for years as your children grow up.

2. **How long have you sold family trips?** The longer the better, of course. Ask for references from families who had kids your children's age when they traveled.

3. **How do you do your research?** The best agents will have personal, up-to-date knowledge. They will vouch personally for the trips they suggest. They won't just tell you that a hotel has a baby-sitting service—they'll also know what those baby-sitters' qualifications are. They will be able to answer your questions easily about the availability of cribs and other baby supplies at a given hotel, the ability to childproof hotel rooms, and the quality and suitability of any children's programs you ask about.

Good agents may also work through specialized family travel operations, ones that serve the family travel niche exclusively and who can be booked through your agent at no extra charge.

FOR MORE INFORMATION:

Family Travel Times is a quarterly newsletter that provides thorough, timely information on specific travel destinations for families. A $40 subscription also includes a call-in service for enthusiastic and personal consultation on any travel-related topic you care to discuss. It isn't a travel agency—they won't book your trip for you—but they will give you all the information you and your travel agent need. Call (212) 477-5524 or write to Travel With Your Children, 40 Fifth Avenue, New York, NY 10011 to subscribe.

Chapter 4
Where to Stay

In America there are two classes of travel—first-class, and with children.—Robert Charles Benchley

Long ago (in the '60s), parents had only one thing to worry about when traveling with their kids: *Does the motel have Magic Fingers?* Savvy parents wouldn't begrudge a dime (later a quarter) dropped into the box by the bed, since they knew that their children would be enthralled by the vibrating mattress for ten minutes or more.

Sadly, hotels that offer Magic Fingers are nearly extinct. But happily, a whole new range of options of where to stay has evolved to take their place.

21. Finding the best hotel for your family

In the 1980s, luxury hotel chains such as Hyatt, Sheraton, Marriott, and Holiday Inn began to advertise special children's programs to attract families, ranging from kids-eat-free promotions, to special children's activities run by hotel staff, to complementary childproofing kits. Unfortunately, the programs offered vary widely among individual hotels in the same chain, making it impossible to recommend one chain over another as being more family-friendly. It depends on where you plan to travel.

If you're in transit and not sure enough about where you'll be staying at night to make reservations ahead of time, go with the hotel that fits your budget. But if you plan to stay a while, and you have time to choose your hotel carefully, here are some questions to help you sort the wheat from the chaff:

1. Do children stay free of charge?
2. Does the hotel offer discounts on adjoining rooms? How much? (Half-price is not uncommon; this question is important if some private time is important, away from your children, and if you feel comfortable using room-to-room monitors to keep in touch.)
3. Does the hotel offer baby-sitting services, or is there an ongoing relationship with an off-site baby-sitting service? What are the qualifications of the staff? How long have they been in business? Can the hotel staff provide long-standing references from the local community? (Minimum requirements include mandatory CPR for all staff members and at least two years' experience with children. In the United States, facilities should also be licensed, bonded, and insured. Assume nothing: Many states waive licensing requirements for facilities where the parent is on-site, such as at a hotel or resort. Also make sure that the facility will take children your child's age. Some will have minimum age requirements as high as six years old.)
4. Does the hotel have an on-site doctor (best), or an arrangement with a clinic near your hotel?
5. Does the hotel have a pool? Does it have a lifeguard on duty? Is it enclosed by a fence or otherwise inaccessible to children? Is it kept at 80 degrees or higher?
6. Does the hotel provide supervised activities for children my children's age? What do they include? What are the qualifications of the staff? (Look for a minimum age of eighteen and at least two years' experience working with children.)

7. Does the hotel's restaurant offer children's meals? What are they?

8. Does the hotel offer cribs, roll-away beds, or other children's supplies at no charge?

9. Will the hotel cooperate with me in childproofing our room? Will they remove all hazardous furniture and objects, including the mini-bar refrigerator? (If you're planning to relax, you don't want a kid-sized refrigerator stocked with intriguing miniature bottles of rum in your room, unless it can be locked. Some hotels will offer to stock your mini-bar instead with nontoxic junk food—perhaps not life-threatening, but even more enticing to your child. Try to get the hotel to agree to remove the unit altogether.)

10. Are the hotel rooms free of nonremovable hazards, such as free-standing radiators, windows that can be tumbled out of, or outside doors without deadbolts within children's reach?

11. What kind of doorknobs does the bathroom have? (You can childproof a regular doorknob, but not a lever-type doorknob. Bathrooms are one of the most hazardous places for children; asking this simple question can save you a lot of jumping up and down to keep your child safe!)

12. Does the hotel have a smoke alarm and sprinkler system? Are there multiple, clearly marked exits from our floor?

13. Does the hotel offer an in-house laundry service?

14. Does the hotel offer in-room cooking facilities and/or refrigeration facilities?

15. Does the hotel offer any other benefits that are important to your family?

If you get five or more positive answers to these questions, you're probably doing very well; more than that and you've found a gem. Your chances of getting a family-friendly hotel go up exponentially as you contact larger, well-known, and more expensive hotel chains, and as you get closer to real tourist destinations where competition for hotel guests is fierce. A good family travel agent should also be able to help you find hotels that provide many or most of the above services.

22. How to childproof your room

One of the most exhausting things about traveling with tots is the way you have to run after them all the time, pulling them away from potentially life-threatening situations. It's not something you'll want to be spending your vacation doing. Although you can't childproof the whole world, you can make your hotel room a safe haven where you'll finally have the chance to stop and catch your breath, even if your children keep on going.

The danger starts early—even infants can squirm, wriggle, and roll off of high places with incredible speed. The hazards increase as your child becomes actively mobile, and decrease somewhat as your child learns to judge height and distance, and to understand that some things are dangerous and to be avoided. Here's a list of what to do for children at each age to make sure your hotel room is safe:

FOR INFANTS (precrawl stage): Common accidents for children under six months are crib accidents, falling from changing tables, and falling out of infant safety seats.

1. If you're using a hotel crib, check it carefully. Look for the Consumer Product Safety Commission label that indicates the crib conforms to CPSC standards. The slats should be no more than 2⅜ inches apart—if you can get a Coke can through, they're too wide. Examine the crib carefully for chipping paint, and rub your hands along all surfaces to check for possible cracks or rough edges.

   The mattress should be firm and should fit snugly. Press down on it to check its support system. Check the drop sides, to make sure that your baby can't release them herself. Get under the crib to check that it has been assembled properly.

   Check the location of the crib. Is it somewhere safe
in the room, with hazards such as windows, sash cords,
and radiators out of reach? Move it to the safest place
in the room.

2. You'll need to create a safe space for changing your
   baby's diaper that takes into account your baby's ability to wriggle off high places. A waterproof pad on the
   floor might do, as long as it's comfortable and convenient for you. Choose one spot in the room to use for
   the entire stay, and make sure that it's free of hazards
   such as electric outlets or other dangers.

3. If you use your safety seat from the car as a place for
   your child to sit up before she can do it on her own,
   make sure that the seat is on the floor or in another
   safe, low area where it won't be knocked over. Always
   belt your child into the seat.

FOR MOBILE TOTS: From eight months to about two years (for
some children even longer), you'll need to worry about your
child's exploration accidents (falling from a climb, bumping into
sharp corners, falling into unguarded water hazards), grabbing
accidents (pulling down heavy objects, grabbing hot coffee), and
accidental ingestion of poisons, since everything your child can
reach has the strong potential of ending up in her mouth. For
your peace of mind, invest some time in choosing a hotel that
cooperates with childproofing. Some hotels even provide guests
with childproofing kits for their rooms. Here are some other hints:

1. Bring a childproofing kit that includes electrical outlet
   covers (12), doorknob covers (3), and a ball of string,
   yarn, or handful of pipe cleaners (all useful for tying up
   drape cords or tying cabinets closed); a foldable safety
   gate; and activated charcoal or syrup of ipecac to give
   your child if she swallows poisonous but noncaustic
   substances.

2. Check the room for unacceptable hazards, and change
   rooms if you need to. If the windows open or if there

is a balcony, choose a room on the first floor. Don't trust window screens—they can be pushed out by the weight of your child.

3. If it is an older hotel (built before 1978, when lead in paint was banned), inspect the walls for cracks and potential paint chip hazards, and ask to see another room if you're dissatisfied.

4. If you can, choose a room with low-shag, wall-to-wall carpeting. Avoid rooms with carpets that are a deep shag that can hide pins, coins, and other choking hazards.

5. Check the room for any hazards that you can remove, including lamps that can be pulled down, a television on a stand or cart, coffee tables with sharp edges, indoor plants that are potentially toxic, and throw rugs on slippery surfaces. Check the cabinets, tabletops, and drawers in each room for small objects that might be found by your child, and remove them.

   When you're through, ask hotel staff to remove the hazards you've identified. Then get down on your hands and knees and tour the room from your children's perspective, to see if there's anything you've missed.

6. For hazards you can't get rid of, you'll want to eliminate access. Install covers over electrical outlets. Check the drapes for loose cords (a strangulation hazard) and double them up so they're out of your child's reach. Put a child-safe doorknob cover on the bathroom door. If there is a kitchen in your room, take the knobs off the stove if they're within your child's reach, and replace them only when you need them. Check for electrical cords that may cause a hazard and remove them. Check for and remove poisonous materials from lower kitchen cabinets.

7. If you know there is a balcony in your room before you get there, be prepared by bringing protective screening with you, to protect your child from getting caught in the bars. Install it immediately.

8. Create a permanent diaper-changing area that is free from hazards within your child's reach. If no other surfaces are appropriate, set up a place on the floor.

9. If your child still uses a crib, check it thoroughly, as suggested in the above section for infants. If she is in a cot or folding bed, check it for safe assembly and make sure that it is free from hinges that can pinch her fingers.

A few minutes' time spent on childproofing your room will pay off in hours of relaxation, where your child can feel free to explore happily, and you can feel free to let her.

FOR OLDER CHILDREN: Just because your child has outgrown the need to put everything into her mouth doesn't mean you can relax. Here are some tips to keep your older child safe in your hotel room:

1. Check the above lists for childproofing tips that still apply, given your child's development and temperament.

2. If your active child likes to climb, bring protective screening for balconies, and make sure to remove furniture or other tempting climbing targets located near your room's windows. Never trust window screens to keep your child safe.

3. Make sure that the room you select has a door that can be latched or closed so that your child can't open it without your knowledge.

4. Talk with your child about safety. Make mandatory safety rules one of the many lessons you teach your child while on vacation.

FOR MORE INFORMATION:

The U.S. Consumer Product Safety Commission publishes a pamphlet on crib safety, available at (800) 638-2772.

23. Condominium rentals, home rentals, and home exchanges

The advantages of renting a condominium or home, or arranging a home exchange with another family, are obvious. You'll get more room to spread out, a kitchen, and some privacy from your children in the evenings when you want it. You can often get better rates than hotels in the same area—home exchanges are essentially free after you pay a one-time annual membership fee to a home exchange organization.

What you usually give up are housekeeping services and other hotel amenities such as pools and restaurants (although in condominium complexes that are built as vacation rentals, even these amenities are available).

When deciding to rent a home or condominium, it's safer to go through an agency than to reply directly to an ad placed by the homeowner, but you will also probably end up paying slightly more than a direct rental. Some agencies are listed below; many others advertise in travel magazines. Ask how long an agency has been in business before using their services.

Home-exchange services compile names of people willing to swap houses, usually for at least two weeks, sometimes for much longer. For a fee usually ranging from $50 to $100, home-exchange services will list your home in an annual catalog, and will send you a copy of the catalog so that you can contact a compatible-sounding family. You can also arrange a trade on your own.

Home exchanges are a gamble—no home-exchange agency actually guarantees that its listings are accurate—but the gamble can pay off with free lodging for your entire trip. There are other special advantages to young families: With a little work, you can exchange with a family that has children the same age, and stay in a home that's been childproofed already; your exchange family may also be able to direct you to their own baby-sitters and to other children in the neighborhood for yours to play with.

To get the most out of a home exchange, start early, at least six months before your planned departure date. If you're flexible about when and where you travel, you have all the more reason to believe you'll find a house that meets your needs.

Take time to correspond with the family you propose to exchange with. Iron out the details of who pays for what—be it phone bills, utilities, or the family car. It's best to get these agreements in writing before you commit.

FOR MORE INFORMATION:

At Home Abroad, 405 E. 56th St., New York, NY 10022; (212) 421-9165, rents properties in Europe, the Caribbean, and Mexico, many of which are suitable for young children.

Country Cottages specializes in vacation rentals in all of the United Kingdom, Ireland, and France. 600 Fairway D., Suite 101B, Deerfield Beach, FL 33441. (800) 674-8883.

The French Experience, 370 Lexington Ave., New York, NY 10017; (212) 986-1115, books *gites*—rustic cottages—throughout rural France.

Heritage of England, P.O. Box 297, Falls Village, CT 06031; (800) 533-5405, handles cottages throughout England, Scotland, and Wales.

Twelve Islands & Beyond, 5431 MacArthur Blvd. NW, Washington, DC 20016; (800) 345-8236, has rentals on the Greek islands.

The two biggest and best-known guides for home exchanges are put out by **Vacation Exchange Club**, (800) 638-3841, and **Intervac**, (800) 756-4663. Neither service vouches for the listings, so do your homework before you agree to a swap.

24. All-inclusive resorts, tours, and cruises

Your first challenge when looking for an all-inclusive resort or tour is finding one that accepts young children—the majority will have minimum age requirements that start around six. Club Med, (800) CLUB-MED, often touted as a forerunner in family-friendly resorts, has no facilities for children under four months, and only a handful for children under two. They additionally offer child-care services in the daytime only, leaving parents to scramble for their own baby-sitters after hours. (To their credit, however, they screen "Baby-Club" and "Mini-Club" employees carefully for child-care expertise, and offer an on-site pediatrician.)

Family-oriented resorts that welcome very young children are gaining ground, however. You will need to work with a specialized family travel agent to get the latest information, and to ask other parents who have stayed at a resort what they think of the children's services. When you find an all-inclusive resort that really does include your children, it can be a stress-free way to spend your vacation, not necessarily more costly than putting a comparable trip together yourself.

If you prefer traveling around to staying in one place, you can still get plenty of help from the travel industry. "F.I.T" is tourist-industry jargon for "fully-inclusive tour." Most tours will have a minimum age requirement. Tour operators will tend to be risk-averse, making them ideal for families who are equally careful, and stifling for more adventurous types. Look for tours that not only accept, but that also welcome young children.

You can even pay a premium for a specialist to arrange a custom tour for your family alone. The tour can offer as much support as you need to have a stress-free trip, including ticketing, reservations at family-friendly establishments, baby-sitting services, and even a twenty-four-hour guide to go along with you if you want. Operators that specialize in F.I.T. packages for families are listed below.

Biking, hiking, or educational tours that welcome children under six are few and far between. Not all trips billed as family adventures will really be appropriate for your children. You can get a better feel for a tour by asking how many children will be coming along, what their ages will be, what activities will be planned for them, and the pace that they will be expected to keep.

Cruises are an all-inclusive resort that floats, and many of the same smart-shopping techniques apply. The cruise industry has gone through a period of rabid competition for the family market, and each line brings out new family offerings nearly every year. There are roughly six thousand cruises each year, to just about any port in the world, so when considering a cruise, it's best to work with a travel agent that specializes in cruises only.

You'll find that all-inclusive vacations will fall into two distinct categories: vacations where your kids are entertained for you, while you go do something else; and vacations where the details like lodging, transportation, and meals are completely taken care of, so that you can relax and be together with your kids as much as possible. Make sure that you choose the type of vacation package that meets your need for separateness or togetherness with your children.

FOR MORE INFORMATION:

The following operators specialize in F.I.T. tours for families.

Family Explorations, at (800) WE-GO-TOO, will arrange tours for families on a custom basis, which can be designed with children under six in mind. Family Explorations also offers guided tours for groups of three to six families, where one staff person will be sent along to manage separate activities for children.

Great Destinations/Families Welcome specializes in creating all-inclusive itineraries for families traveling to Europe, complete with accommodations that welcome young families, baby-sitting services, and tours that include age-appropriate activities for your children. (800) 326-0724.

Rascals in Paradise is a tour packager that is especially good at tracking down upscale, family-friendly resorts at international seaside destinations; it will also design custom itineraries for families. (800) U-RASCAL.

Traveling Families is a full-service travel agency that will put together detailed itineraries for families, or will find a resort that is geared for families at the destination of your choice. Full of ideas. (800) 225-1300.

25. Renting what you don't bring

If you find you can't do without a high chair, playpen, or other major baby item, check first to see if your hotel will supply it for free. Some hotels will go out of their way to fulfill special requests, particularly in areas with intense competition for guests. They could be ready to provide you everything from high chairs to cribs to strollers to room monitors, and more.

If not, check to see if your hotel will rent supplies to you, or can help you to get in touch with a local rental agency. Family-friendly establishments will be used to this kind of request, and will have numbers available for you to call. If you are renting a condominium or house, you can contact Baby's Away, a baby supply franchise that is particularly strong in ski resort areas, at (800) 571-0077. Baby's Away has been known to help parents locate convenient rental locations, even if they themselves don't have an outlet close enough to help you.

Chapter 5

Managing Meals

Even if you plan to rent a room with kitchen facilities, you'll want a break from cooking sometimes. When you eat out with your kids, choose a place where you can enjoy each other's company as well as the food.

Don't let a few bad experiences sour you on restaurant meals with your children. Most kids will learn to love the elegant ritual of ordering a meal, having it arrive, eating, and waiting for Mom or Dad to pay the check, but they need to see it a few times to understand it. Soon they'll anticipate a visit to the restaurant with excitement, and will feel proud to be included.

26. Best-bet restaurants

Don't assume that a children's menu means you've found a child-friendly restaurant. For very young children, it's more a bid for the parents' business than any obvious perk for your child. What's on the menu is also not particularly important for children as young as yours—you can bring their food along with you, or you can almost always order something for yourself that they can eat, too.

So what *is* important? Contrary to popular belief, you don't have to stick with the so-called "family restaurants" to have a good time. But do look for these things:

Fast turnaround. Family restaurants with glacial service can give your kids all the crayons and free placemats to color in the world, but your children will still be unhappy if the food doesn't come on time. Pick places where you can be in and out in forty-five minutes or less. You can stay longer, of course, if all goes well, but that will be up to you. **Bright acoustics.** Choose high-ceilinged, open restaurants full of hard surfaces that bounce the sound around. Such a layout encourages loud talking anyway, and your children's voices will blend right in instead of intruding on the pleasure of other diners.

For babies, the above two requirements are the only ones you need to worry about. Just bring the infant safety seat in with you from the car (or a stroller, if the restaurant permits), and time your visit so that you get there just after a feeding and/or when your child is likely to want to sleep.

From eight months on, look for places that also satisfy these two additional requirements:

Lots of room. Choose restaurants that give you and your kids the space you need, whether it be a larger table than usual, aisles wide enough to bring a stroller in, or an outdoor seating area where boisterous and whiny kids just don't seem to be as annoying as they would be indoors. **Entertainment value.** Choose restaurants where your kids have more to do than just wait for you to finish eating. Make sure to judge the entertainment quotient from your children's point of view. Skip the view restaurants, and choose instead anywhere that offers live music, has an open kitchen, features an aquarium in the lobby, or at the very least has Crêpes Suzette on the dessert menu, so you can order a spectacular flaming thing to arrive at your table just when your children are about to wilt.

Quick service, bright acoustics, lots of room, and entertainment value—it sounds like McDonald's, right? Well, yes. But it also does a good job of describing plenty of other choices, if you let your imagination go. Like sushi bars, which are fast, noisy, with plenty of action. Or new Italian restaurants—pasta is quick to the table, and new places tend to be decorated in hardwood and brass, reflecting sound nicely. Or Asian steakhouses, where your dinner is cooked in front of you with a flash of knives. Or microbreweries. Or pizza joints. Your choices are endless, as long as you stick to places that satisfy the above four criteria.

27. Fifteen questions to ask a restaurant, before you make the reservation

If you plan to spend a lot of money for a special meal, do some more research on how child-friendly a restaurant really is. Once you've picked some likely candidates from the Yellow Pages or your concierge's recommended list, call them, and whenever possible, choose restaurants that answer *yes* to these questions:

1. Do you have meals on the menu that you'll guarantee to serve in fifteen minutes or less after we order?

   Slow service is the kiss of death for any night out with the kids. Your children's attention spans won't tolerate it, and neither should you.

2. Will you allow me to bring my own food for my kids?

   Look for an enthusiastic "yes," followed by an offer to warm food or formula if needed.

3. Do you take advance orders, so the food will be ready when we arrive?

4. Do you have free breadsticks?

   If your children range in age anywhere from seven months to seven years, a good bread basket will add a good fifteen minutes of quiet contentment to your mealtime.

5. Do you have wide aisles between tables?

   Wide aisles help you navigate strollers more easily, give you and your toddlers some elbow room, and protect other diners from flying food and/or the direct impact of a noisy child. Children also seem to like a little space and to behave better when they get it. Some restaurants don't allow strollers inside, so if you're planning to use one, be sure to ask.

6. Will you give me a booth or table large enough for four to six adults, even if there are only two adults in my group?

An important question if your children are of an age where they like to grab anything, including your plate, and throw it on the floor. (And their reach is inhumanly long, as any parent can attest.) If the restaurant has high chairs with their own trays, this question is far less important, but many restaurants stock high chairs that are meant to be pushed up to the table itself.

7. Would you say that your restaurant has an active atmosphere, with a healthy decibel level?

8. Can we order à la carte, and can we change our order to take-out if we need to leave early?

Most restaurants will say "yes," but look for ones that say so enthusiastically, or that offer meals that travel well in a doggy bag.

9. Do you have high chairs and booster seats?

Obviously a "no" answer is a strong indication that the restaurant doesn't want family business—except outside of North America, when you'll be lucky to find a high chair anywhere you dine.

10. Do you supply changing tables in the men's and women's rooms?

Restaurants could make it so much easier for parents than they do. The cost for these tables is so little—approximately $200 to $300, with installation adding another $100 or so—it's a wonder that more restaurants haven't provided them. Those that supply changing tables in both men's and women's rooms are definitely in the minority, though, making those that say "yes" to this question the definite cream of the crop. (One intrepid father insists that changing tables aren't necessary, by the way—if there isn't any horizontal space in the men's room, he takes the lid off of a toilet tank, suspends it between two sinks, and changes the baby there. His wife recommends a "don't ask, don't tell" policy when handing a baby to its father to be changed in a men's room.)

Look for a *no* answer to the following questions:

1. Do you use tablecloths on your tables?

    The "grab" factor from six months to two years or so needs to be reckoned with, and tablecloths are, from your child's point of view, just made to be yanked off the table. Along with your dinner.
2. Is your smoking section larger than your nonsmoking section?

    The more space devoted to smokers, the less likely a restaurant is interested in children. In the United States, the answer to this question should grow more and more obvious as cities and counties follow a national trend to ban smoking in restaurants—but until then, it's important to ask.
3. Would you describe your restaurant atmosphere as being "quiet" and/or "intimate"?

    Save these restaurants for the night when you hire a baby-sitter.
4. Do you have any preference about what time my family makes our reservation?

    It's something of a trick question. You'll probably *want* to dine early. But the customer is always right, and that means you, not the restaurant, should decide when to come. If the person you're speaking with responds enthusiastically with a suggestion that you come in before five, she's more interested in the other diners than in your family's needs.
5. Do you reserve a section of your restaurant for families with children?

Just because you have children doesn't mean you want to sit with everybody else's. Choose restaurants that seat you and your family along with other diners, instead of treating children like they need to be quarantined.

28. Fifteen ways to increase your chances of enjoying your restaurant meal

1. Buy a very nice bottle of wine. Leave it in your hotel room.
2. Choose a restaurant where a fine meal can be ordered, enjoyed, and concluded in forty-five minutes.
3. Make reservations at a time when your infant, if you have one, is most likely to sleep through the meal.
4. Dine at off-peak hours, so that the staff will have time to be attentive.
5. Forget the advice about asking to be put in a corner away from the hubbub—ask to be seated at tables where there's a lot of action. For example, sit where your children have a view of the kitchen or the front door.
6. Ask for an extra-large table if your child is at an age where she likes to grab things. Ask for a booth if your child is too old to be strapped in, but too young to sit still—seat her on the inside of the booth next to the wall.
7. Order as soon as you sit down, or better yet, ask the restaurant to fax a menu to your hotel, and order ahead of time.
8. Order meals that you can eat with one hand, so that you can hold a child in your lap if you need to, even after your meal comes.
9. Order meals from the buffet table, or meals that take ten minutes or less to prepare and that will taste good even if you have to eat it from a plastic container after you get back to the hotel.
10. Forget courses—ask for everything to be brought at once. Eat first the things that you'd like to enjoy hot.

Have your salad last, in other words. The French do
it that way all the time.

11. Keep children out of their booster seats or high
chairs, and in your lap or wherever makes them most
happy, until your meals come.

12. If your children are very active and restless, accommodate them. Just after you complete your order,
plan to take a very short walk with them, whether it
be to visit the rest room, to look at the pictures in the
lobby, or to stroll around the parking lot until the
food arrives. There's no rule saying that you or they
have to sit and wait at the table, with nothing to do
but stare at the salt shakers.

13. If your child is still in the messy-eater stage, bring her
bib, spill-proof cup, and a suction-bottomed bowl, as
well as food she likes in case she rejects the restaurant fare. A bowl that your child can't drop on the
floor is particularly important, to avoid a big mess
around your table.

14. Bring a good supply of disposable, pre-moistened
wipes to clean high chairs and other surfaces before
your child uses them.

15. If you meet with an untimely tantrum, ask your
server to pack up your food. Take the kids back to
your hotel, and be with them until they go to sleep.
Then open your wine and give yourselves a toast.
Enjoy your food. And don't feel defeated. Try going
out again as soon as you can: The more you take your
children out to restaurants, the better they'll get at it,
and the more they'll learn to anticipate and enjoy the
experience with you.

29. When you have a kitchen (how to avoid becoming its slave)

Renting a room with a kitchen is a great convenience, yes. It
will save you money, undoubtedly. It's a tremendous way to
avoid the uncertainties and the potential high drama of dining

out with small children. And there are probably a few people out there who will actually enjoy spending their vacations shopping for food, cooking meals, and washing dishes three times a day.

For the rest of us, we'll want to spend as little time in the kitchen as possible while on vacation, and as much time as possible having fun with our family. Here are some ways to make sure you don't become a slave to your stove:

1. If traveling with your spouse, agree before you leave on who will be responsible for the planning, shopping, cooking, and cleaning required during your trip, for each and every meal.

2. Plan your menus carefully. Choose dinner menus that freeze well and take a half-hour or less to prepare. Plan lunch menus that can be packed easily and taken along. And plan breakfast menus that require no cooking at all, for example, yogurt and fruit, or cereals. Don't count on introducing any new foods to your children at this time. Stick to the tried-and-true favorites, to make mealtimes as smooth as possible.

3. Pack a survival kit of staples, things you know you'll need and won't want to buy since you'll never use them up. Some suggestions: dishwashing liquid, salt, pepper, favorite spices (garlic powder and nice herb blends go a long way), oil, and vinegar. Bring plastic stuff for the kids, and kitchen items that may be missing that you don't want to do without: possibly, dish towels, can opener, bottle opener, corkscrew, utility knife, picnic basket, thermos, and ice chest.

4. If your destination is close by, make as many meals as you can ahead of time, freeze them, and bring them along. Make an exhaustive grocery list that covers your entire menu plan. If you can't freeze your food and bring it with you, then shop once for everything you need when you get there, cook it all at once, and freeze meals when you're there to be ready when you need them.

Chapter 6
Foot Traffic

The swiftest traveler is he that goes afoot.
—Henry David Thoreau

There are three facts that you need to keep in mind about walking around with your children:

- Your children's legs are much shorter than yours.
- Your children are heavier than they look.
- You'll be doing a lot more walking than you think.

These facts make it imperative that you strategize ahead of time about how you'll walk around with your young children. Your options include child carriers, strollers, and letting them get there on their own steam—keeping in mind, of course, their shorter legs and staying power.

30. Choosing a child carrier for your vacation

Until your child can walk, and before she gets too heavy to carry, your best bet for making sure that she enjoys your vacation as much as you do is to invest in and to use a child carrier.

When you put your child into a stroller, she becomes a spectator. She's down near the ground, away from the action. Most significant, she is far away from you.

When you carry your child along as you walk, she becomes a participant. She's at eye-level with the world, seeing what you see. She can talk and sing with you and feel your closeness. A child carrier will allow you to take your child with you wherever you go, whereas strollers will keep you confined to paved and relatively level paths.

Carriers are also safer than strollers. Your child is next to your body, so you are well aware of any potential dangers in her environment. Stroller-related accidents each year nearly match accidents caused by baby walkers or portable gates.

There are a few disadvantages to using a child carrier to completely replace your stroller. With a child carrier, you are still bearing the full weight of your child, no matter how cleverly a well-designed carrier distributes that weight. That fact makes carriers impractical beyond the point where your child is greater than about one-quarter of your body weight. Another disadvantage is that you can only carry one of your children at a time. And a carrier can be hot for your baby in warm climates. But the advantages so far outweigh the disadvantages that it's wise to invest in a carrier for your travels, even if you've not used one before.

Child carriers vary greatly from one another in design and construction. Some designs have been used by women for thousands of years; others are very new. Choosing the best one will depend on your build, your child's age and weight, and what makes both of you feel comfortable. What works wonderfully for one child and parent might be completely uncomfortable for others, so be prepared to experiment, and to change to another carrier as your child grows. Here are your options on styles:

1. **A sling-type carrier.** The carrier is worn over one shoulder, creating a hammocklike space for your child. Newborns can snuggle next to you for a womblike experience. Older children can sit cross-legged or on one of your hips to see out. You and your child will either hate or love this design—there seems to be no middle ground whatsoever. Manufacturers claim slings

can be used for children up to forty-five pounds, but
they are best for children under twenty pounds.

2. **A front-carrier.** The carrier suspends your child's
weight from your shoulders; the child is carried on
your chest. Some designs are for newborns only, who
are carried facing you, with strong neck support built
into the design. Others can be converted to allow your
child to face out and see the world. Because the
weight of your child is usually suspended on your
shoulders alone, look for designs with well-padded
shoulder straps and don't expect to use even the best
designed front-carriers after your child reaches
twenty-five pounds.

3. **A backpack-style carrier.** Framed backpack-style
carriers are a boon for outdoor travelers. A well-
designed, well-fitted carrier will be comfortable for
children up to thirty-five pounds. Be careful, though,
not to use it when your child weighs so much, in pro-
portion to your own size, that she will be able to throw
you off balance if she moves abruptly. Backpack-style
carriers with frames are also not appropriate before six
months of age, since children need to be able to hold
their heads up well on their own.

4. **Innovative designs.** A number of entrepreneurial
moms, dissatisfied with the commercial child carriers
that are widely available, have marketed their own
designs and made these available via mail order. Not
surprisingly, many of these products mimic age-old,
mother-tested designs from traditional cultures,
where babies are often carried for their first few years
of life. If retail selections available in your area don't
meet your needs, look for alternatives advertised in
parenting magazines, or contact suppliers listed below.

FOR MORE INFORMATION:

The following child carriers each offer unique features for a
family's travel needs, and are also not always widely available in

retail outlets. If the regular retail products you can find in your area don't satisfy you, consider the following solutions, listed in alphabetical order:

Antelope Mountain Sports Baby Backpacks. Offers framed backpack-style carriers. Unlike other backpack-style carriers, Antelope Mountain Sports carriers are made to order. If you have a narrower or broader torso than the normal range for commercial products, or if you have found that other products are for some other reason uncomfortable, this product offers a custom-fit alternative. The company also markets an adapter kit to convert your own backpack. For serious hikers, backpackers, and hard-to-fit parents, who have children over six months who can hold their heads up well. Mail order: (408) 364-1772.

Baby Bundler. Based on an age-old design, the Baby Bundler resembles an extremely long receiving blanket (about six yards!), made from a soft cotton-knit blend with a finely finished edge. It comes with instructions, including a videotape, showing parents how to tie the baby on comfortably and securely. Because it is free of straps, buckles, or other paraphernalia, it is easy to pack. The simple design offers parents the choice of carrying the child in front or back. The Bundler distributes a child's weight so well over your shoulders, hips, and torso that you can carry a much larger child in front than with other carriers. Many children and parents prefer the front-carry position because of its increased intimacy. Baby Bundler will fit almost everyone, from very small frames up to three hundred pounds. The manufacturer will also make extra-large products on request. Available in some retail outlets in Oregon, or via mail order at (800) 253-3502.

Baby Trekker. A very heavy-duty front-carrier, with well-padded shoulder straps and a strong hip belt to distribute your child's weight more efficiently than other carriers do. Babies can face in or out. It's a good alternative for parents and children who like a front-carrier, but find their child has grown too heavy for carriers where the child's entire weight is carried by the parent's shoulders. A parent can also use the Baby Trekker to carry a child in back. Mail order only, from Pettersen Infant Products: (800) 665-3957.

Baby Wrap. Based on an African design, the Baby Wrap is a soft, strapless carrier that wraps around your entire torso; none of your child's weight is carried by your shoulders. Best for children who can hold their heads up well; not so good for large-breasted women. Available in two sizes, by mail order only: (800) 432-0494.

New Native Carrier. A sling-type carrier that, unlike other sling-type products, comes in multiple sizes. Instead of the O-ring adjustment found on other slings, the New Native Carrier is a single circle of cloth that packs flat. Good for hard-to-fit parents who like the sling design, especially parents with smaller frames that feel overwhelmed by "one-size-fits-all" slings. Mail order only: (800) 646-1682.

Remond Handy-Chair Child Carrier. Something like carrying a small chair for your child on your back. Unlike most other backpack-style carriers, your child faces backward, which is somewhat safer and gives her 180-degree visibility. Two other nice features for travel: The design is stable enough to be used as a chair as well as a carrier, and it folds flat. Mail order: (800) 426-9244.

31. Choosing a stroller for your vacation

Strollers are preferable to carriers when your child is uncomfortably heavy for you, when you have a bad back or other health limitations that make carrying your child difficult, or when you're carrying other things, for example, to help you get through airports. You'll also find a stroller a necessity when your small children outnumber you (such as multiple-birth children), when multipassenger strollers can be a godsend.

The safety record for strollers isn't very good. Brakes fail, children's arms and legs get pinched, and children fall out of strollers at an alarming rate, particularly with cheaper models. Before you make a final selection, check with the U.S. Consumer Product

Safety Commission at (800) 638-2772 to make sure it's safe.

Once a model meets general safety requirements, look for these features:

1. **The lighter, the better.** Your travel stroller should weigh under ten pounds, preferably under eight. Every pound will make a difference, after a few times lugging it out of the trunk or up a flight of stairs.
2. **Ease of maneuvering.** Look for double wheels in front and back, and for models that fold easily.
3. **Comfort for you and baby.** The handles should adjust for your height. The seat should be comfortable enough for your child to sleep in, and offer sun and rain protection.

You will usually need to make a trade-off between comfort for your child and the weight of the stroller. When making that trade-off, ask yourself how you'll be using the stroller. Do you expect your child to be in the stroller for naps, or at restaurants that don't have high chairs? Or is it a tandem stroller, that you'll use for more than one child at a time? In those circumstances, it's worth it to get a stroller that's a little heavier but that offers more comfort for your children. Umbrella-type strollers offer less comfort and safety for your child than full-feature strollers, but are also more portable.

What about jogging strollers? Although they can travel more rugged terrain than traditional or umbrella-type strollers, their need for increased stability means that they are heavy. And they're not really maneuverable, making them a poor choice for travel. Stick to jogging with them; substituting a child carrier for a stroller will allow you to carry your children to even more rugged terrain with far less equipment.

32. Keeping older children happy and safe while walking around

What about a child who is too old for either a carrier or a stroller? Here are some rules to keep in mind:

1. Figure that your three-year-old child is good for a half-mile of walking at most in a day. That's about ten short city blocks. And that means, realistically, only about a quarter-mile of actual distance covered, since a lot of your child's walking power will be used up in running around in circles, or away from you. Increase your estimate of how far your child should be expected to walk by no more than an additional half-mile per year of age.

2. Even if a distance seems an easy walk to you, always look for alternative modes of transportation besides walking to get there. Even a simple taxi ride will be a great adventure for your child. Be on the alert for any opportunity to ride on weird escalators, moving walkways, glass elevators, elevated trains, or subways to get to your destination. You'll make getting there less of a chore and more of an adventure.

3. If your child wants to be independent but still can't be trusted in crowds or traffic, invest in a safety harness and tether. If you or your child don't like the look of a harness, you can choose instead a wrist strap, which is less obtrusive, but still keeps your walking toddler within arm's length. For older children you can alternatively get a specially-designed, mobile electronic monitoring system, one that looks like a pager and will alert you if your child wanders farther than a few feet away from you.

4. You can't really expect a child this age to memorize the phone number where you're staying, even if she can remember your home number. Plan instead to pin your child's name, home address, and hotel telephone number on her clothes. Teach her to stay in one place if she loses sight of you, and not to go away with strangers even if they say they know you.

Chapter 7
When Getting There Is All the Fun

For my part, I travel not to go anywhere, but to go.
I travel for travel's sake. The great affair is to move.
—Robert Louis Stevenson

33. The Zen of road trips

Road trips are an American tradition, and a good vacation alternative for families with young children. Most babies love riding in a car so much that it's a recommended remedy for colic. Most older children adapt quickly to road trips. And, especially if you tie your own tent to the roof of the car, no trip can give you as much freedom to roam as getting in your car, backing out of your driveway, and seeing where the road takes you and your children.

Even if your goal is to get somewhere and stay there, try to make the drive itself a special part of your vacation. If you do, you'll never hear the words "are we there yet?" from the backseat of your car. Here are some ways to turn conventional wisdom about driving with children on its head, and to make your drive enjoyable for everyone in the process:

Conventional wisdom: Leave at night, when the kids are asleep.

Why it's wrong: You get tired, the kids sleep fitfully, and worst of all, you arrive at your hotel several hours before check-in time.

The Zen way: Leave when you're ready. Make the trip a part of your vacation instead of something to avoid—your vacation starts when you lock the front door.

Conventional wisdom: Drive until you get there.

Why it's wrong: You get competitive and tense about how far you've come, and how fast. You get tired, and so do your children.

The Zen way: Take frequent rest stops, at least twenty minutes after every two hours of driving, to unwind and to let your children run around. Expect to stop more frequently the younger your children are.

Conventional wisdom: The adults decide when to stop and when their children must use the rest room.

Why it's wrong: They won't need to go when you want them to.

The Zen way: Ask your children to help you with the rest stop schedule, as soon as they're old enough to understand. Show them where you're going on the map, and ask them for their input about how far to travel before stopping again. Stop when your children need you to.

Conventional wisdom: Don't drive for more than four hours a day when you're traveling with children.

Why it's wrong: It isn't wrong. It's a great idea. Better yet, plan an itinerary where you don't drive for longer than two hours a day.

34. Keeping your children happy on the road

Given that only a few generations ago American children were walking for thousands of miles on the Oregon Trail and other points west, on trips that took many months to complete, it's amazing how much we fret about our kids getting bored during a simple car trip. Children are extremely adaptable, if nothing else. Although the first day of a long trip can be difficult, your children will tend after that to become accustomed to the rhythm of the road. Here are some ways to make that transition very easy for them and for you:

1. **Respect your children's natural rhythms.** Small infants will need to be changed and fed as often as every hour, so plan a twenty-minute stop for every hour of driving. You may not need to stop so often— she may decide to sleep through the day—but by expecting to stop that often, you won't be tense about it when it happens.

2. **Tell your children what to expect.** Even very young children can understand what you tell them, more than we think. Take time to explain how long the drive will be, in terms they'll understand. Show them where you're going on the map, and give them frequent updates on your progress.

3. **Give them responsibility for their own entertainment.** Let your children select their own toys and games to bring. Books on tape are an excellent alternative from about the age of three on—buy each of your children her own tape player and headphones. It may not do wonders for family togetherness, but it will keep your children quietly occupied when they begin to get restless.

4. **Be with them.** Be flexible with your seating arrangements. If you have an air bag on the passenger side of the front seat, never seat a child there—it isn't safe. But if you don't, then give your children a new view by changing everyone's seat around every once in a while. Or join your children in the backseat when it isn't your turn to drive. They'll feel less isolated and they'll enjoy your physical closeness.

5. **Remember that you're driving.** Don't ever forget that you're behind the wheel and that you're hurtling your family forward at tremendous speeds. If your children must scream, fight, wail, and whine, then let them do just that until you can pull over safely. Don't respond until you've had time to put your car into "park" and to stop the engine. Above all, resist the temptation to take them out of their safety seats to feed them or comfort them as you drive along. Always stop first.

FOR MORE INFORMATION:

The National Highway Traffic Safety Administration Auto Safety Hotline at (800) 424-9393 provides information on product recalls and safe installation of child safety seats. **Safety Belt Safe USA** at (800) 745-SAFE provides similar information.

Wimmer Ferguson, (800) 747-2454, makes travel toys for even your youngest children, specially designed for road trips.

The American Academy of Pediatrics publishes a brochure entitled "The Family Guide to Car Seats," available by calling (800) 433-9016. Updated annually, it provides recommendations of brands and models as well as safe installation practices.

35. What to do about motion sickness

When you were a child, you probably didn't ride in a car seat, so you may have been riding too low to get a good view out the window. Your parents may have given you books to read in the car to keep you content. They may have told you, lovingly and unknowingly, to lie down in the backseat to take a nap when you were tired. They may even have smoked in the car. No wonder you remember throwing up a lot—all of these things are sure recipes for a very unhappy tummy.

Fortunately, we know better now.

Motion sickness seems to affect small children more often than adults or infants—perhaps because adults have accustomed themselves to travel-related motion, and infants are still used to the womb, where notions of up and down don't exist.

Here are the best ways to make a child who is prone to motion sickness more comfortable on long car rides:

1. Let her look out the window. Make sure to buy child safety seats that are high enough for your child to see out. Built-in safety seats, in particular, seem to be too low for many children. When a child can see the same motion that her body feels, she is far less likely to be ill.

2. Seat her facing forward. Putting the child safety seat in the forward-facing position will also be less likely to cause nausea, although you should obviously not opt for this position until your child is developmentally ready (the American Academy of Pediatrics recommends not to use the forward-facing position until your child is at least twenty pounds and at least one year of age).

3. Don't let her read. Don't allow your child to look at books in the car, or to play with toys that require her to look inside rather than outside. Buy her a cassette recorder and provide books-on-tape for kids instead to amuse her, or play games with her that require her to look outside a lot.

4. Don't smoke in the car. Also don't subject your child to food odors that she finds unpleasant. Respect her wishes if she complains about a smell, and get rid of the offending object, even if you can't smell it. Children's senses of smell and taste are very keen.

5. Don't feed your child spicy or greasy foods while traveling. But do give her something bland to eat before you drive—a little food in her stomach will actually calm things down.

6. Take rest stops at frequent intervals, and stop when your child feels very uncomfortable. Sometimes a two-minute walk is all that's needed to relieve nausea.

7. Bring ginger capsules and fresh mint. Herbalists claim that chewing on a leaf of fresh mint or eating ginger can bring instant relief for a sour stomach. Some children's stomachs also are soothed by a soft drink.

8. Use acupressure. The acupressure point to relieve nausea is in the middle of the meaty portion of your child's hand, between the thumb and forefinger. Press the spot firmly with your own thumb and forefinger, right at the base of the "V" formed by the bones connecting your child's thumb with the rest of her hand.

9. Avoid over-the-counter drugs. Since over-the-counter remedies don't usually include dosages for small children and might cause harmful side effects, motion sickness medicine should be prescribed by your child's pediatrician. It needs to be taken hours before any symptoms occur, so it should be used only if you know from experience that your child will become uncomfortable without it.

36. Domestic train travel

Train travel with children can be wonderful or miserable. It's wonderful when your children are old enough to love it, when you spend the money to go in style, and when you don't overdo it. It's miserable when you want to get somewhere and are trying to save money by sleeping in the cheap seats.

A short journey by train can be a magical experience for a child who is just entering the phase of being fascinated by different modes of transportation. Don't make the mistake of thinking that "passenger train" equals "Amtrak" in the United States. There are over two hundred privately-owned passenger lines, many of which cover stunningly scenic routes or that offer rides in lovingly preserved Pullman cars pulled by turn-of-the-century steam engines. There's the Grand Canyon Railway line, (800) 843-8724, for example, which offers a sixty-five-mile, steam-engine–driven ride through some of Arizona's best scenery. Or the Santa Cruz, Big Trees and Pacific Railway, (408) 335-4484, a day's drive south of San Francisco, which offers a narrow-gauge steam train journey from the Santa Cruz Mountains to the Pacific Ocean. The Steam Passenger Service Directory gives detailed listings on all the short lines in the United States, as well as information about dozens of railroad and trolley museums, and can be ordered by calling (800) 356-0246.

Amtrak has made a special effort to make their trips more appealing to families. The Coast Starlight, which runs between Los Angeles and Seattle, even employs mimes, musicians, and magicians to keep the kids happy.

But sitting up all night is still just as miserable as ever. If you decide to travel overnight on Amtrak, be ready to go first-class, to book yourself a sleeping car, and to pay for the privilege: Sitting up with young children in a public car all night does not for a vacation make. Also, ask *not* to be put in a Heritage car. These older cars are designed so that the beds need to be raised in order to use the toilet facilities. The newer Viewliner cars don't have this design flaw. Amtrak can be reached by calling (800) USA-RAIL.

37. Twenty more ways to get there that your children will love

Remember that if your children are over eighteen months or so, they've entered the age where weird modes of transportation rank high on their list of great things to do, right up there with anything to do with water and going to visit big, ugly animals. Take every opportunity to introduce a little fun into your transportation methods, and take the time to let your kids enjoy themselves in transit. Better yet, make transportation the goal of your day trip. Walk over bridges and watch the boats go by. Visit a fire station to see the fire engines. Stop at the mass transit museum. Go to the biggest train station in town. Here's an alphabetical list, to get you started, of even more transportation modes that your child will love:

1. airplanes (private)
2. boats of any kind
3. cable cars
4. cog railways
5. computerized rapid transit
6. double-decker buses

7. escalators
8. ferries
9. glass elevators
10. helicopters
11. horse-drawn carriages
12. hydrofoils
13. light rail systems
14. limousines
15. monorails
16. moving sidewalks
17. narrow-gauge railroads
18. subways
19. taxis
20. tow trucks (even if your car breaks down, your kids will have fun riding back in it to the garage!)

Chapter 8
The Not-So-Friendly Skies: Air Travel with Small Children

Q: Where do you suggest I change my baby's diaper?

A: I'm sorry, but we don't have facilities for that type of procedure on this aircraft.

—mother and flight attendant, San Francisco to Newark

If it takes a village to raise a child, then you've entered the territory of a hostile tribe the moment you set foot on an airplane. Fellow passengers and sometimes even the flight crew itself can treat you with active animosity. Much of that animosity comes from the fact that modern air travel almost by definition is an uncivilizing experience: cramped, crowded, and claustrophobic.

There are very few rules for flying with children under five. Here they are:

1. **You can't sit in emergency rows.** Children under sixteen are prohibited by the Federal Aviation Administration (FAA) from sitting in emergency rows.

2. **You can bring child safety seats.** The FAA also mandates that domestic carriers must accept child safety seats designed for automobile travel, whenever the seats bear labels stating conformity with federal safety standards. Booster seats and harness restraints, however, have been declared hazardous by the FAA and are banned from use. The FAA recommends not using a safety seat once your child has reached forty pounds. Use the regular seat belt instead. There are, unfortunately, no safety seats on the market that are designed expressly for air travel.

3. **Your child can fly on your lap.** Children under two and under forty pounds may fly on the lap of an accompanying adult, according to the FAA. Most airlines stipulate only one lap child per paying passenger.

4. **You can't give dirty diapers to flight attendants.** As with any other food-serving establishment, the Food and Drug Administration (FDA) mandates that flight attendants may not handle garbage, including dirty diapers, when serving food. After changing fifty to eighty diapers a week for a while, you may forget that you're handling human waste. Don't be upset if the flight attendant reacts in horror if you try to hand her a dirty diaper, no matter how neatly you've stowed it in an airsick bag.

Beyond these rules, you're pretty much at the mercy of the gate attendants and the flight crew. Your experience may vary greatly from flight to flight, even when flying with the same carrier. The trick is to stay calm, to ask for help aggressively when you need it, and to keep your child as safe and as comfortable as possible. Here's how.

38. Why you should buy all of your children tickets

All domestic carriers allow you to fly with your children under two seated on your lap free of charge. International flights offer discounts for lap children, who usually fly for 10 percent of the regular fare. The FAA maintains that mandating tickets for children under two will raise the cost of air travel, and will force families with young children to travel by car instead. Since car travel is far more dangerous than air travel, such a mandate may even raise the injury rate for children, something the FAA wants to avoid.

Despite the current FAA stance, buying all of your children their own tickets, no matter what their age, makes good sense.

When your child has her own seat, you can use her child safety seat from your car to restrain her. Currently these seats offer the best protection for your children. Imagine being in an emergency, where your child is the only thing in the cabin that is not secure. People in the airline industry have been known to call lap children "missiles." Any legal restraint will be better than nothing at all.

Child safety seats aren't just a good idea in an emergency. Accidents are rare. Turbulence isn't. By buckling your child in, you will greatly reduce the risk of injury when your plane hits a rough patch of air.

Then there are the softer issues. Imagine what it will be like to hold your child in your lap for more than a very short flight. It will be impractical to eat or to read, difficult to move about, and unpleasant for both of you. It can increase your tension. Children get their emotional cues from you. Is it worth the cost of a seat to start your trip with everyone in a bad mood?

39. Making the journey as safe as possible

Whether or not you purchase a ticket for your child under two, do bring a child safety seat with you to the gate for any child who is less than four years of age or forty pounds (when they reach this age and weight, they can sit in the seat using the adult safety belt). If there are empty seats it may be possible to seat your child without purchasing a ticket.

Note that the label on your child's safety seat stating that it is approved for use on an airplane doesn't guarantee that it will actually fit in economy-class seats. Measure your child's safety seat before your trip. If it is wider than seventeen inches, the width of a standard economy-class seat, then you won't be able to use it in the economy cabin. Upgrade your ticket, or buy a narrower child safety seat before flying.

In crash tests conducted by the FAA, booster seats and harness devices were found to be a hazard to children, and have been banned. Forward-facing seats were found to provide limited, but useful protection. Rear-facing seats were found to be the most effective. Use the rear-facing position whenever possible with your child.

When deciding whether a child can sit in a rear-facing seat in the plane, the most useful measure is not weight, but height: If the child can still sit comfortably when in a rear-facing seat, with her head below the back of the seat, then it will provide better protection than a forward-facing seat. If your child's safety seat can be used in either a forward or rear-facing position, always opt for installing it rear-facing for take-off and landing, if your child isn't yet too tall for this position.

Pay attention to the safety demonstration. Locate the exits, and count the number of rows between your seats and the nearest exit so that you'll be able to feel your way to them in the event that the cabin fills with smoke. Wear flat shoes, don't wear pantyhose (extremely flammable), and dress your children in brightly-colored, flame-retardant clothing.

40. How to get a seat for your child even if you don't pay for one

If you can't afford to buy a ticket for your child under two, you can nevertheless greatly increase your odds of having an empty seat next to you for your child to use. There are too many people involved in the seat assignment process—from airline reservation clerks, to travel agents, to passengers booking their own flights on on-line systems, to the flight crew itself—for you to absolutely guarantee that the below methods will work. But for your child's safety and comfort, they are definitely worth a try:

1. Fly at light times. Ask your travel agent to help you with finding the least-busy flights for your particular route.

In general, plan to travel on a Tuesday, Wednesday, or Saturday, in the very early morning or after 7 P.M. These flights tend to be less full, increasing your chances of finding a seat for your child. A side benefit is that flights on these days and times are also usually less expensive. You also want to be sure whenever possible that your flight originates from your departure point. Otherwise, travelers on the first leg of the journey will have first crack at the seats.

2. Reserve split seats. If traveling with another adult or another child who is over two, reserve a window and an aisle seat in the same row. Ask the reservation agent to flag your reservation, indicating that you'll also have a lap child with you. You want to increase the chances that other agents won't use the middle seat in your row for another passenger's reservation.

3. Arrive early, about one and a half hours before a domestic flight, and two and a half hours for an international flight. If the middle seat in your row is still open, then remind the attendant at the front desk that you're traveling with a lap child, and ask her politely to keep the seat open for as long as possible. If the seat has been assigned, politely ask the attendant if she can page the passenger in that seat, so she can ask the passenger to move to another available seat.

4. Talk to the gate attendants. Attendants at the gate may also be making last-minute seat assignments. If so, then get in line again at the gate and ask them for their cooperation in keeping the seat available or in moving a passenger who has been assigned the seat.

5. Bring each child a safety seat. Even if you don't have a seat for your child yet, bring your child's safety seat with you to the gate, along with a large plastic garbage bag. If there absolutely isn't a place in the airplane for your child except your lap, and you're convinced of that, put the safety seat into the garbage bag to protect it from getting dirty and give it to the flight attendants

to check through to the baggage compartment. Rear-facing infant seats designed for children up to twenty pounds will fit in your overhead compartment and won't need to be checked.

6. If traveling alone with your child, reserve a window seat. Most airlines will allow child safety seats to be used only in window seats. When installed anywhere else these seats are considered a safety hazard, since they'll block passengers in that row from leaving the plane in an emergency. If the middle seat stays open, sit in it yourself and put your child in the window seat you reserved.

7. Ask the flight crew. Even after the seat has been assigned, and even after boarding, you may still be able to work with the flight crew to get a seat for your child. Ask for help as you board in moving the passenger next to you to a new seat if one is available. Be brief—otherwise you'll be holding up the line and no one will want to help you.

8. Ask your neighbor. If someone comes to claim the seat next to you, don't be shy about politely asking her if she would mind moving to another seat should one become available. Often the passenger will be all too glad to get away and will actively help you search out alternatives. Often even a "fully booked" plane will have empty seats at takeoff, so keep your eyes open.

9. Be nice. Like the best salesperson, be nice, but be ruthless, too. Make sure that everyone likes you and wants to help, but don't stop asking until you get to "yes." Even the best salesperson knows when to quit, though. Remember that you're asking for something for nothing; the only way to absolutely guarantee a seat for your child is to buy one.

41. Where to sit

The rule that says you should fly in the best class of service that you can comfortably afford doesn't really apply when traveling with children. Many of the amenities in first-class or business-class are lost on children. What's worse, you may not be able to enjoy them, either. Many parents have felt decidedly not welcome outside of the economy berths. Although your flight may be very pleasant, parents are also sometimes asked to leave first-class and to take their children to the back of the plane to calm them down. If your children are at a restless age and broad social censure disturbs you, then fly economy-class.

Bulkhead seats (seats in the row just behind first-class) have more legroom than other economy seats, enough to put a baby in an umbrella stroller in front of you. They also have the advantage of having no seats in front of them for your children to kick the backs of—and other passengers seem willing to forgive anything of your child besides having their seats kicked.

But you can't always reserve these seats. Many airlines have adopted a policy of allowing only wheelchair passengers to make advanced reservations of bulkhead seats. Other airlines follow a secretive policy of setting these seats aside for their preferred customers only. Still others don't seat families anywhere in the first *eight* rows of economy-class, to give their first-class customers the best possible chance of not being disturbed by your children.

These rules seem to change more frequently than the people making your reservation can keep up with. Sometimes you will be assured that you're in the bulkhead row, only to find when you get to the airport that your seat reservation has been canceled and you can't even find seats together, much less in the row of your choice. Sometimes you'll be told that those seats aren't available to children unless you go to the airport early to claim them, and you'll end up again without seats together, when some other family beats you to the punch.

If you still want to try for bulkhead seats, make your reservation as early as possible, and call back after you've purchased your ticket to make sure you still have the seat assignments. Don't ever take the suggestion of waiting for seat assignments until you get to the airport. If the person taking your reservation won't give you bulkhead seats over the phone, then reserve another row.

Be sure to be explicit when making your reservation about your plans to travel with children, and be certain that your seat assignments aren't inadvertently made in an exit row. If traveling with children under sixteen, you'll be asked to move, and will again face the prospect of being split up.

42. Making it to the gate

If you are traveling with another adult, it's good to divide the labor, with one adult solely responsible for keeping the kids safe and happy, and the other solely responsible for waiting in lines, handling the tickets and carry-on baggage, and managing any last-minute problems. Some airports have security precautions that require all passengers to be identified when checking in; if so, one adult can wait in a quiet area with the children until the other reaches the head of the line.

If you're the only adult in your party, air travel will be particularly challenging. Bring or hire help, or make sure that you can manage everything easily yourself, including your baby or babies. Use a carry-on bag that is especially made for frequent travelers that has wheels and a retractable handle that allows you to pull it easily from waist level. With this type of bag, you can manage one infant in a front-carrier, and one or more in a stroller, depending on the stroller's capacity. Plan to check your stroller at the gate, and ask for it to be delivered to the gate when you arrive.

Once you streamline your method for carrying your personal items, carry-on bag, and your children, the big problem that's left to be solved is how to manage child safety seats for one or more children. These are heavy and cumbersome, and simply not made for easy transport through an airport terminal. A convertible stroller–child safety seat combination is a good solution, as it will allow you to wheel one child all the way to the gate in her safety seat. Another alternative is a portable, folding car seat that meets federal regulations for safety. The Guardian Folder is one alternative, available from The Right Start at (800) 548-8531. It's expensive ($149.95), but convenient if you plan to travel often.

Some airlines have family lounges in their hub airports; Air France, for example, maintains areas for families in the JFK Airport in New York, and in the DeGaulle airport in Paris. Many airports also maintain their own special areas for families traveling with any airline, complete with childproof furniture, a changing area, and a play area to let your kids tire themselves out a little before a long flight.

These family lounges are extremely common in major domestic airports, but are not well advertised, and are inexplicably hard to find without help. Your best bet is to call the airport in advance. Ask the operator for assistance on which department handles the family lounge or nursery areas of the airport—usually it will be the custodial department.

43. What to do about ear pain

When the pilot adjusts the pressure of the cabin during descent, your children may experience severe ear pain. Enthusiastic sucking, chewing, and swallowing can relieve it. If your child is breast-feeding, take her out of her seat to nurse only if she is clearly uncomfortable, since you will lose the safety benefits of having her buckled in. Try to ease her back into her seat after nursing relieves her ears.

If you are feeding formula or if your child sometimes drinks juice from a bottle, try to have your baby accustomed to drinking all of these cold. There is no medical reason for heating formula. Descent is a busy time for flight attendants, and you won't be able to count on getting your baby's bottle warmed up at that time.

For older children, pack something that requires a lot of chewing. Obviously gum and hard candy—favorite remedies for ear pain for adults—aren't appropriate for children under five. An uncut bagel might be just right, or an orange segment. If your children are old enough to play games, ask them to make faces with you, and to imitate you opening your mouth very wide. Start the game about the time you start descending, not when your child has already exhibited signs of discomfort.

Handkerchiefs or paper towels immersed in hot water, placed into the bottom of plastic or Styrofoam cups, and held to your children's ears can completely clear up ear pain, almost magically. But flight attendants may be too busy to help you during the descent itself. So if you are deeply concerned about ear pain or have experienced problems in the past with your child, plan ahead by carrying a small thermos and handkerchiefs of your own. Ask the flight attendant to fill the thermos with hot water and to provide you with cups just before you begin your descent.

44. What to do about colds, ear infections, teething pain, and immunization reactions

For a simple cold, your child won't get better any sooner by staying home. Most children are less bothered by their colds than their parents are. But if your child has a stuffy head, do follow the procedures above to minimize ear pain during descent.

Ask your pediatrician whether she recommends a decongestant for someone your child's age, to be taken two hours before descent. Air travel is already a dehydrating experience, though, so don't use a decongestant unless your child is very uncomfortable. In either case, make sure your sick child drinks plenty of liquids during the flight.

Ear infections are a more serious matter. For some children, they are extremely painful. Even with treatment (acetaminophen for typical viral ear infections, and antibiotics for bacterial infections), your child will be uncomfortable for about four days. You'll need to determine for yourself if the flight you've planned is still a good idea; your decision might be based on whether your child has just been diagnosed or is over the worst.

The Eustachian tube, which equalizes pressure in the middle ear, may be blocked during ear infections, which can cause more pain than usual during descent. It can also cause possible (but unlikely) damage to the eardrum. You can minimize the risk to your children's ears by asking your doctor for a decongestant for your child, and by following the procedures for ear pain recommended above.

Children aren't prone to teething on schedule, so don't try to plan your trip around the date of a tooth's most likely emergence. If teething, your children won't only be in a bad mood: Another symptom that is particularly irksome for air travel is diarrhea. If she is teething, be prepared by taking along a diaper for every half-hour of your planned flight time.

One of the best teethers for travel is a large handkerchief or bandanna, since it packs small and can be used for other things, too. Ask the flight attendant for ice water, tie a large knot in the handkerchief, dip it into the water, and wring it out until almost dry before giving it to your baby.

Unlike teething, immunizations are usually on a schedule. Common side effects of some immunizations include fever and marked irritability. Schedule your vacation around your baby's immunization schedule whenever possible to avoid needing to soothe your child through the worst while on a crowded plane.

45. Managing meals for you and your children

If you are flying with a child in your lap, you'll definitely need to refuel yourself by eating, but you won't be able to manage a hot food tray easily unless traveling with another adult. Ask if the airline offers a brown-bag meal. You'll need to order it twenty-four hours in advance. A cold sandwich and fruit will not only be easier to eat than a hot meal, it will also likely be your most nutritious alternative.

Typical U.S. airline fare is too salty, too overcooked, and too processed to be healthful. Ordering special meals can help: The regular fare is often prepared by airline caterers weeks or days in advance, then frozen, whereas special meal orders are often made up only hours in advance. If you prefer a hot meal to a brown-bag meal, and you aren't a vegetarian, then opt for "kosher" or "low-salt" menus. Vegetarian meals are often just a double serving of the regular meal's bread and vegetables without the meat.

Children's meals are equally dismal in the nutrition category, but if your child is old enough to eat them (two or older) then they can provide an interesting diversion. Your child may genuinely enjoy the experience of being served a little tray of food, no matter how tasteless, rather than eating yet another sandwich from your carry-on bag. Order the meal twenty-four hours in advance of your flight. Some carriers also offer "infant" meals of strained commercial baby food.

But come prepared to feed yourselves, in any case. Some carriers don't serve more than a packet of honey peanuts for anything shorter than a three-hour flight; if you're taking connecting flights you may get nuts the whole way. Bagels are a good flight food as soon as your child is old enough to eat them, as are juices, squares of cheese, and fruit and vegetable cubes—steam these ahead of time to a consistency that your child can manage easily. Store them in leak-proof containers in your carry-on and serve them as finger food.

If your baby drinks formula, then the convenience of pre-mixed formula is probably worth the extra weight in your carry-on bag. Some flight attendants will heat formula in the galley microwave, and some won't. It's best to accustom your baby ahead of time to drinking cold formula. If an attendant does agree to heat a bottle for you, be very careful to check its temperature, as the galley is not really set up for that kind of thing.

If you're breast-feeding, close quarters can make you and fellow passengers more sensitive than usual about what should be the most natural thing in the world. The best advice? Do what comes naturally between you and your baby, and don't worry about it. Discreet nursing is difficult to manage in economy-class, even with the most cooperative baby.

If you feel uncomfortably exposed, however, you can increase your feeling of privacy by sitting in the window seat, temporarily moving your child's safety seat to the middle row, and draping a blanket over the safety seat to form a partial barrier. (You won't be able to do this during ascent or descent, however, when the child safety seat must be next to the window.) You can also stuff a pillow between your seat and the next one, which will give you a little more privacy from the row behind you.

46. On-board diaper changing strategies

New airplanes such as 757s have changing tables in every lavatory, but since planes are often kept in service for twenty years or longer, you won't be able to count on flying in a plane with changing tables until your child has graduated not only from diapers but maybe even from college, too.

If you're on a flight without changing tables, the best place to change your child's diaper will depend on a delicate balance of three factors: what's actually in the diaper, how old your child is, and how much you care about the opinion of strangers sharing the nearby rows with you. Here are your best options:

1. **Your tray table.** The advantages are, it's relatively sanitary, it's at exactly the right level when you're sitting down, and it will hold a child's weight easily up to about thirty pounds. If your child is too long for one tray table, the adjoining one can be lowered to double your work area. Disadvantages include these: You need to be quick. You're exposed, so to speak, so you risk social censure if it's too messy a job. And older kids might rebel.

2. **Your seat, plus the adjoining seat.** The advantages are the same as your tray table, only it offers a larger work area and is lower, giving your child more privacy if she is at a stage where she cares. Disadvantages? You need to stand up and work from the aisle, so it's very clear to everyone what you're doing, and you get in other people's way. It's not really possible to maneuver on a single seat, so you also need the cooperation of a fellow passenger.

3. **The lavatory.** To make an acceptable changing area, take three airline blankets plus a changing pad into the lavatory with you. Close the toilet seat. Roll up two blankets to level out the area around the toilet seat to a more or less flat surface, and put the third one over the top, plus the changing pad. Perform the change. The main advantage of this method is that it's private.

There are two disadvantages. First, the surface of the toilet is slippery plastic, and it's hard to hang on to your baby if she is squirmy or if you hit a patch of turbulence. You can get around this by also taking along a rubber-backed piece of flannel, such as those sold to protect your baby's crib mattress or bassinet; putting this down first on the toilet seat will give you some traction. A second, more troubling disadvantage is that, even with a lot of blankets under your baby, the lavatory isn't a very pleasant or sanitary place after a few hours into a flight.

If you have bulkhead seats, the floor in front of you is also an option. Remember, though, that if you decide to change your baby in the cabin instead of the lavatory, you shouldn't expect a flight attendant to take a dirty disposable diaper from you, especially when food is being served. FDA health regulations prohibit them from helping you at that time. Pack the diaper neatly in an airsick bag. Dispose of it yourself in a lavatory trash receptacle, or take it with you when you leave the plane.

47. Keeping your children happy on long flights

In many cases, the smaller your infant, the better traveler she will be. The constant hum of the engines has a soothing effect on most infants. Don't, however, plan to travel by air before she is a week old: Changes in air pressure may cause problems in very small infants, especially if their lungs are not fully expanded.

When not sleeping, your small baby will most likely be interested in eating. Expect her to want to nurse more frequently than usual, both for comfort in a strange situation, and because of the dehydration she'll experience on long flights. If your child is formula-fed, have an ample supply handy to handle both her increased needs and any unexpected delays. Be as self-sufficient as possible. Getting a bottle heated is an iffy prospect at best—some flight attendants just won't. Get your baby accustomed to cold formula before the flight.

Keeping your eight-month- to three-year-old child happy on long flights will be a challenge. If possible, fly at night, when most children this age will be happy to sleep for the duration of the journey, especially when in their familiar car seat. If you fly by day, then be mentally prepared to spend all of your energy entertaining and comforting your child.

Pack a number of new toys. Good travel toys for children this age are books, finger puppets, pop-up toys, toys with moving parts and if possible a rubber suction cup that will keep them mounted to the tray table, and anything else that encourages interactive play. Count on needing to pack one new toy for about every hour of your flight.

You'll want to think small, of course, but children under three tend to put things into their mouths, so make sure the toys you select are choke-proof. Safety First, in Massachusetts at (617) 964-7744, sells the No-Choke Testing Tube, similar to the device used by the government and toy manufacturers to test toys for children under three years of age. It's worth taking along. Another good, readily available alternative that errs on the safe side is a toilet paper roll: if the toy fits into the roll, it's too small for your baby.

If your toddler is at the stage where dropping things is a very good game, seat her in a rear-facing safety seat next to the window, and stuff the area between the seat and the window with pillows to block dropped toys from disappearing forever.

When your toddler is awake, you are likely going to need all of your energy to keep her active mind busy and happy. Count on really playing with her for as long as the flight lasts—not just distracting her with a toy so you can finish a magazine article. Carrying her around the cabin every once in a while, especially to look for other children, is a good break for both of you from trying to keep her happy in her seat.

Expect air travel with children this age to be challenging. Your child will go through at least one stage of lung-testing before she understands what "quiet, please" means, and that stage might come mid-flight. Once she's mastered the skill of moving around on her own, she simply won't be happy to sit still for long periods. Nor would you want her to. Don't expect too much from your child, and don't stress yourself unnecessarily about whether she is bothering other passengers by her age-appropriate behaviors.

At some point, probably after three years of age, your child will be old enough to entertain herself quietly for at least some portion of the flight, and to understand that making a lot of noise is not okay, if you tell her it isn't. Your child will also be old enough to understand that you're going up in the air on a journey. Talk to her ahead of time about what to expect, and involve her in the selection of favorite books and toys to take along. Take time during the flight to explain to her what is going on, and to answer her questions.

Some three- to five-year-old children will be very content to listen to books on tape, making a portable cassette recorder a great investment in your piece of mind. Coloring books are also a good alternative. And pack plenty of new, compact toys to take out as surprises during the journey. Many parents like to wrap these in colorful paper, since children this age delight in unwrapping gifts.

48. If your children won't settle down

What if your children simply won't settle down and be quiet? What then?

First, remind yourself that many behaviors, such as crying, fidgeting, and complaining when uncomfortable, are completely appropriate for a child, however annoying they may be to adults. The stress of air travel may make your child more irritable or more needy than usual, and that, too, is perfectly normal behavior, even if it adds to the discomfort of fellow passengers.

If you have done everything you can to comfort your child and tend to her needs, and she is still very unhappy, then remind yourself that the flight will eventually end. Try to not worry about what others think. You'll never see them again, after all, and your child will be your child forever.

If you are very, very worried about disturbing others or causing your child unnecessary stress, then your pediatrician may agree to prescribe antihistamines for your child to make her drowsy on the flight. You'll be drugging your child for no medical reason, though. Also be aware that these drugs will cause hyperactivity, not drowsiness, in a significant number of children, which will increase your troubles instead of alleviating them.

FOR MORE INFORMATION:

You can order "Going on an Airplane," written by Fred Rogers of *Mr. Roger's Neighborhood*, through your local bookstore or by contacting **Family Communications**, 4802 Fifth Ave., Pittsburgh, PA 15213.

A tip sheet for consumers about traveling with children is available from the **FAA** at (800) FAA-SURE. It also can be downloaded as a text file, childtip.txt, from Library 13 of CompuServe's Travel Forum, or from the FAA's data library in the FedWorld data base, which is accessible via the Internet at ftp.fedworld.gov or at www.fedworld.gov.

49. What to do about jet lag

Children's circadian rhythms tend to adapt themselves to new time zones with much greater ease than their parents'. The best thing to do about your children's jet lag is to not worry about it too much. See that they get a lot of rest before your trip, don't try to adjust their schedule before you leave, make sure that they drink plenty of liquids on the plane, and plan for a few easy days to rest and adjust when you arrive.

Try to arrive when it's early evening in the new time zone, giving yourselves and your children enough time to travel to your hotel, eat a leisurely meal, and have a nice bath before bedtime. Plan to put your children to bed at their usual time, no matter what the "real" time is for them. If you're sharing a room, be sure to dim the lights to give their bodies a chance to realize it's night; better yet, turn the lights off altogether and go to sleep at the same time yourself.

What about your own jet lag? The more you can do to be well-rested, the better you'll be able to handle the inevitable surprises that come with being a traveling parent. While nothing is a sure cure, here are some potential preventives that are worth trying:

1. Eat high-protein, low-fat meals during the journey and a few days before you leave.
2. Avoid caffeine and alcohol, but drink plenty of other liquids during the journey, especially water.
3. Several recent studies indicate that doses of synthetic melatonin can help your body clock fight the disorienting effects of time-zone changes. Melatonin capsules are readily available at health-food shops.
4. For a few days before you leave, you can also gradually shift your own periods of eating, sleeping, and waking to more closely correspond with the new time zone.

FOR MORE INFORMATION:

"Defeating Jet Lag" is a free pamphlet that provides a diet regimen. To obtain it, send a stamped, self-addressed no. 10 envelope to the Forsyth Travel Library, 9154 W. 57th St., P.O. Box 2975, Shawnee Mission, KS 66201.

Chapter 9
Special Situations

Just about anything with your kids can classify as a "special situation," of course. But some special situations are more common than others. Here are a few that you might encounter in your family travels and travails.

50. Weekend trips

We often start the weekend with high hopes of spending some quality time with our children, yet reach the end of it wondering when we'll ever find the time to really pay attention to them. Dual-career families have often meant the death of leisure time, and weekends become the time where we do all the work around the house that we don't have time for during the week.

Getting yourself and your spouse out of the habit of working seven days a week, and into the habit of taking family trips, will take some planning. Start by unplugging your TV—the average American household spends about one-third of its weekend in front of a television set. Then organize: Schedule chores with your spouse to be done during the week, or do them one weekend so you'll have time to travel on the next.

Try to reserve every Saturday morning for a day trip with your family. Morning outings can include visiting local fairs and museums, hiking in nearby parks, or visits to friends and relatives.

Although your town may not be a tourist attraction, remember that everything is new and exciting to your child. Many of the things that your children will enjoy most at this age are also free: a visit to a local fire station, for example, or to the library.

If you start early, you can get home by noon and do whatever chores you need to at that time. If you make it a habit to reserve each Saturday morning for such an outing, then you won't ever again ask yourself on Sunday night, "Why didn't I have time for my kids again this weekend?"

51. Combining business and family travel

It can be done. Really. As a matter of fact, roughly one-sixth of business trips also include some element of family travel along with them. As the number of women in business grows, you can expect the number of business trips with kids to grow, too.

Are you taking the kids on your own? Then you'll need someone to care for them while you're doing business. Assuming that your company is not yet enlightened enough to pay for your fly-along nanny, here are the three most convenient methods for finding child care:

1. **Your hotel.** Select a hotel that has on-site care, or that has a standing agreement with a baby-sitting agency that is licensed, bonded, and insured. Ask for references, and check them.
2. **Your company.** If you're visiting a company location with on-site day care, or a corporate contract with a day-care facility, ask if the site can accommodate your child for the duration of your visit.
3. **Your customers.** Ask the business associates whom you're visiting for a personal recommendation of a sitter they've used for their own children.

If you plan to stay a few extra days with your family when your work is done, try to select a single hotel for your entire trip, rather than move to a new location once the trip is on your own tab rather than the company's. The hassle of moving to a

new location once your children have had time to accustom
themselves to the old one is rarely worth the dollars you save.

It will take some research to find a hotel that will cater both
to your business needs and your family's preferences. At the
very least, make sure your hotel allows children to stay for free,
that room windows can't be opened, and that rooms lock from
the inside and have a deadbolt that small children can't reach.
And finally, before booking, remember any special needs you
might have, such as a refrigerator to store breast milk, or supplies such as cribs, strollers, and high chairs, which some hotels
will provide for free.

52. When you're a single parent

The term "single parent" includes widows and widowers,
divorced custodial and noncustodial parents, single parents by
choice who have conceived or adopted a child on their own,
and gay parents who are in a committed relationship and aren't
really "single" at all. Single parents do have some things in
common, though. Usually they are torn between spending time
with their kids and providing for them. And more often than
not, they underestimate their own needs when it comes to
planning family vacations.

However much you want this time to be for you and your
kids alone, don't forget that you're an adult, and may need
adult company, not only for the chance to have a conversation
that's not about Barney, but also to help you with the logistics
of vacationing with small children. It could be as casual as vacationing with another single parent who has children the same
age as your own. Or as elaborate as joining a group tour that's
especially geared for single-parent families.

If organized vacations make you gag, and you like the idea of
having adult company along both to keep you company and to
help with the kids, don't forget about members of your own
extended family as potential travel partners. Some parents are
so locked into the nuclear-family model of vacationing that
they forget to consider other relatives as suitable travel companions. If you vacation with your own parents, for example,

your children will get the added advantage of spending time with their grandparents, and you have caregivers along who love your children nearly as much as you do.

A few years ago, the travel industry had travel packages for "singles," a good place to snag a mate or at least have a great time with members of the opposite sex—and travel packages for "families," tailor-made for the model family that included both a mom and a dad. People like you, people who were both "single" and "family," fell through the cracks. That's no longer the case. A good travel agent should be able to direct you to vacation alternatives that are aimed solely at one adult traveling with children.

A good single-parent vacation package will do away with the "singles supplement"—the surcharge of 50 percent to 100 percent that is regularly tacked onto the bill when a single adult signs up for a vacation that is usually meant for "double occupancy." The package should provide age-appropriate activities for your children, and a chance for you to unwind with other single parents. Some will provide you the opportunity to save money by sharing accommodations with another adult and child on the same tour. Look for tour operators who regularly advertise rates for "one adult, one child" in their brochures, and ask about the marital status of the parents and the ages of the children for a given tour, to make sure that both you and your children will feel at home.

Are you planning international travel with your children? Before you go, ask the embassy or consulate of your destination country whether you need notarized authorization from your children's other parent, even if you're the custodial parent. Such permission is required of single adults traveling with children to many countries, including Australia, Brazil, and Mexico.

FOR MORE INFORMATION:

Local single-parent groups are often good resources for vacation partners or for organized tours. A good place to start is **Parents Without Partners**, a national group with local chapters in many areas of the United States. A spokesperson at the national headquarters estimates that about 25 percent of the organization's activities are trip-related. Call (800) 637-7974 for information about chapters near you, or write to them at 401 N. Michigan Ave., Chicago, IL 60611.

Gay and Lesbian Parents Coalition International offers a variety of support services. P.O. Box 50360, Washington, DC 20091; (202) 583-8029.

The National Organization of Single Mothers, P.O. Box 68, Midland, NC 28107-0068; (704) 888-KIDS, offers how-to information for single mothers. For a free copy of *SingleMOTHER* newsletter, send $1 for postage.

53. When you're pregnant

If you're pregnant and traveling, you'll be taking more personal responsibility for your health and for the health of your unborn baby than if you were sitting at home just a phone call away from your doctor. If you're going to be away for an extended period of time and will be missing critical prenatal visits, ask your doctor to refer you to another doctor at your destination.

Be attentive to your nutritional requirements. It's a good time to plan a vacation where you have access to a kitchen, so you'll have plenty of control over what and when you eat. Obviously you'll want to avoid tobacco and alcohol. Remember also to ask for nonsmoking flights if your destination is an international one.

For many women, pregnancy is a time of decreased energy. Make sure your schedule includes plenty of time for naps, if that's what you feel like doing. Your needs will dovetail nicely with the needs of your other children, who will enjoy the company if you decide to sleep in with them during their afternoon nap.

While traveling, avoid sitting still in one place for a long time as much as possible, as it can aggravate such common symptoms of pregnancy as swollen feet and ankles, constipation, or hemorrhoids. Sure, that's easier said than done when you're on an airplane or in a car. But make a point of scheduling frequent breaks to get out of your seat and walk around, and try to sit with your feet raised whenever you can.

Don't travel to destinations where additional immunizations are required or recommended, unless you plan far enough ahead to get these immunizations before you become pregnant. Immunizations can often involve a live virus, never a good idea to introduce into the environment of your growing baby. Even vaccines with dead viruses are risky, since they can cause fever.

When should you go? Most women recommend the second trimester, when you're over the most unpleasant stages of morning sickness and fatigue, and not yet really uncomfortable from carrying your baby. The second trimester is usually also the time when prenatal care is the least critical, since you've passed the danger point for early miscarriage and haven't yet reached the time when you're likely to deliver.

There are a lot of myths when you may or may not be absolutely forbidden to board an aircraft when pregnant. Here's the straight skinny: Tariff 35 of the U.S. Department of Transportation (DOT) allows air carriers to bar you from traveling on their aircraft within one week of your due date, unless you have a signed letter from your doctor saying you've been examined and are in no imminent danger of going into labor within the next seventy-two hours. (Mothers may wonder at the faith the DOT places in doctors for being able to predict just when a woman will go into labor!) Airlines definitely will try to discourage you from traveling in the third trimester at all, for the obvious reason of not wanting you to deliver your baby on the plane. They may have a point, there. But unless you're forthcoming about your due date and it's within a week of your flight time, they can't really keep you off unless you're already in obvious labor.

What about exposure to radiation and its effects on your unborn baby? Ten hours in a plane at 35,000 feet will expose you to about the same level of radiation as a chest X ray. It's difficult to judge what harm, if any, a single round-trip flight will have on your developing baby, but to be on the safe side you may want to delay your flight plans until after the first trimester, when the most critical development occurs. For the latest information, you can contact the High Altitude Radiation Monitoring Service, Inc., at P.O. Box 4204, Stamford, CT 06907.

Have a plan ready if you do go into labor while on vacation, or if you require medical assistance. Check with your doctor before you go on any symptoms that your doctor feels will need medical evaluation immediately. And know what your insurance covers before you go. You don't want to have to second-guess your coverage when you and your baby are in need of emergency medical attention.

54. When last year was a disaster

Too many parents put vacations on hold for years after a single disastrous experience. Maybe they paid a premium for an all-inclusive resort with full-time baby-sitters, then discovered the resort's baby-sitting staff was little more than a collection of bored preteens with no experience. Or they took their children camping, and endured a hellish existence of whining and complaining for days on end. Or their baby simply wouldn't stop crying.

People involved in failed business ventures do a "post-mortem" to find out what went wrong, and how to fix it for the next time. You can do that, too, for vacations that were less than ideal. A postmortem can help you to avoid most or all of the problems you experienced before. The worst thing you can do is decide to vacation in the backyard for the next eighteen years until the kids are gone.

Here are some questions to help you through your very own postmortem:

1. How much could we have avoided the problem, by better planning?
2. How much of the problem has solved itself, simply because our kids have gotten out of the stage they were in before?
3. How much of the problem can be solved by learning to be more flexible, myself, and recognize that vacations with kids don't need to be perfect to be enjoyable?
4. What else would solve the problem, beyond staying at home for the rest of our lives?

The more you can think of specific answers for the particular problems you faced last year, the more confident you will be that this year won't be a repeat performance.

55. When you can't afford a vacation

Once you have children, you'll never seem to have as much money as you used to. But somewhere there's a family with half your income that's managed to put together a wonderful vacation, even on their budget. Don't let money worry you out of what's a magical time for you and your kids: your first five years as a family. There will be a way, even if it's just a few days' camping in a park an hour's drive from your home.

Your three biggest costs on a vacation will be transportation, lodging, and food. Once you decide what your vacation budget is, you can take each of these categories and find ways to reduce your costs until you've planned a vacation that fits your budget. Here are some suggestions:

Transportation:

1. Driving is cheaper.
2. If you fly, make it off-season. Purchase your tickets at least fourteen days in advance. Usually the further in advance you plan, the cheaper your tickets will be. Also be sure to take advantage of discount brokers when investigating airline ticket prices, often advertised in newspaper travel sections.
3. Be flexible about when you leave. Airlines set aside only a set amount of seats on each flight for their lowest available fares. Be flexible about flight times and dates, and keep asking about cheaper alternatives. If you have a good travel agent she should be able to help you through this process.
4. Stay close. The closer to home your destination is, the less expensive your transportation costs will be. If budgets are tight this year, contact your local chamber of commerce and local travel bureaus for vacation ideas close to home.

Lodging:

1. Stay where it's free. The least expensive overnight stays will be a) visits with friends or relatives (free, within reason) or b) camping. If you've never camped before, borrow the equipment you need. Even state and local campsites with complete amenities, including hot showers and electrical hookups, will usually be less than $8 per night. If you prefer a roof over your head to a tent, look for family cabin facilities in state and national parks near your destination.
2. Do without daily maid service and other high-priced amenities of hotels by renting a cheaper condo or private home, one that's large enough to invite another family to share costs with you.
3. Choose nontrendy destinations, where everything will be less expensive. Travel destinations go in and out of fashion. On Oahu, for example, the first Hawaiian island to develop tourism in a big way, you'll pay less for the same services than you will on other islands, simply because it has become less interesting to tourists than less developed destinations. Almost anywhere you've heard of, whether it be a ski resort or a Caribbean isle, will have an inexpensive alternative nearby. Get a guidebook that's geared for student or budget travelers to help you locate these destinations.

Food:

1. Eat in as much as possible, by renting a room with a kitchen. Theoretically, you won't spend any more than you would at home, since you'd have to buy groceries there, too.
2. Go out for breakfast, if you do go out, since it's the least expensive meal.
3. Pack lunch.
4. Shop for dinner bargains. If you do go out for dinner, take advantage of early-bird specials, restaurants that give you big price breaks for eating before five in the

evening. You'll have the added advantage of having fewer diners to worry about bothering, should your children be in a restless mood.

5. Drink the water. The big money wasters when you go out to eat are the beverages. Make up your mind ahead of time to not order any alcohol in restaurants. No double cappuccinos in the morning, either—bring your own espresso machine if you must have it. And if you're really on a strict budget, stick to water with your restaurant meals.

FOR MORE INFORMATION:

Discount brokers are available in many areas of the travel industry, buying blocks of rooms or other travel-related products and selling them to consumers at a discount.

Hotel brokers can secure discounts of as much as 50 percent at good hotels. Try these:

- Hotel Reservations Network (800) 964-6835
- Quikbook (800) 789-9887
- Express Reservations (800) 356-1123
- Central Reservations Service, (800) 950-0232, for Florida, New York, and San Francisco

Cruise brokers include the following:

- Cruises Only (800) 683-7447
- Cruise Line (800) 777-0707
- Cruises of Distinction (800) 634-3445
- Spur-of-the-Moment Cruises (310) 521-1060
- White Travel Service (800) 547-4790
- Dial-a-Cruise (800) 882-9000

Airfare consolidators negotiate with airlines, then pass deals on to you or to your travel agent:

- Unitravel (800) 325-2222

- Jetset (800) 638-3273 or (213) 290-5800
- Euram (800) 848-6789
- Travac (800) 872-8800
- Council Charter (800) 800-8222

56. Coping with sleeping problems

Be respectful of your children's established sleep routines and duplicate them as closely as possible when away from home. Established routines will give your child a sense of comfort even in an unfamiliar place. Make sure that you bring a child's favorite teddy bear or blanket. Make sure that there is a quiet period before you put her to bed every night, no matter how hectic the vacation schedule seems. You may also want to bring a night-light to give your children a sense of familiarity if they wake up at night.

The best way to cope with sleep problems might be to take your children into bed with you, at least for the first several nights away. Your steady breathing will have a calming effect on them, and your familiar presence makes even the strangest of new places feel like home. Even if you aren't used to cosleeping at home, you will usually find that your children readily adapt and are comforted by sleeping with you while away. Don't worry unnecessarily about your children getting so used to the comfort of sleeping in your bed that they don't go back to their own beds when you return home: They will when they're ready, and right now they may need more nurturing from you than usual.

If you or your spouse are very uncomfortable with the notion of sharing your bed, you can transfer your child to her own bed after she's asleep, or you can place an infant's crib next to your bed with the side of the crib folded down, so she knows you're within arm's reach.

57. Coping with eating problems

Motion sickness can cause eating problems while you're in transit. Prevention is the best remedy: To avoid motion sickness in automobiles, keep your child in her safety seat with a clear view of the horizon; crack a window for fresh air if she becomes nauseated. Don't worry too much about feeding your child if she doesn't feel up to it, but do offer cold liquids to avoid dehydration, and ice if the child is old enough. Some drugs provide limited effectiveness against motion sickness, but you will need to check with your doctor on whether they are recommended for children your child's age. You will also need to administer these hours before the onset of symptoms for them to be effective—otherwise your child will likely lose it before it does any good.

Once you've arrived, try to make food as familiar as possible for your child. This will be easy for a breast-fed or bottle-fed infant, but less so for older children, who will be more aware of unfamiliar circumstances and unexpected food flavors. If your older child temporarily loses her appetite because of jet lag or simply as a reaction to unfamiliar territory, try not to be overly worried. Make sure that she gets enough fluids to avoid dehydration as she grows accustomed to her surroundings, particularly in hot climates or after a long plane ride.

58. A special-needs child

If your child has a disability or a chronic disorder, you will need special advice before traveling. Start with your doctor or specialist, then turn to support organizations, many of whom will have members who have already solved the problems that you now may feel are insurmountable.

The Americans with Disabilities Act of 1990 has not only improved matters for travelers needing wheelchair access, it's also marked the beginning of a new kind of tolerance in the United States for travelers of all kinds. You may have challenges to solve on your travels that other parents can't even conceive, but you owe it to yourself and your child to do what you can to overcome them.

Children with special health problems or medical conditions may need specialized restraint systems for travel by automobile. Contact the National Easter Seal Society at (800) 221-6827 and ask about the Kids Are Riding Safe (KARS) program.

Air travel can be especially difficult for children requiring a wheelchair. Speak up—tell people that you will be traveling with a disabled child, and ask what they can do to help. Each airline will have a slightly different procedure, so ask as many questions as you need to, to feel comfortable that your child will be well cared for.

When calling the airline to make reservations, have the dimensions of your child's wheelchair available. Foldable chairs may be allowed in the cabin, making them a good investment if only to avoid the complications that will inevitably follow your request for special handling of a power wheelchair. The airline's ground crew will be responsible for preparing power wheelchairs or scooters for transport. This may or may not include removal of the chair's battery. At your destination, the chair should be ready and waiting for your child at the gate by the time that the other passengers have disembarked.

Security checkpoints at airports can be stressful for your child, who may be requested to get out of her chair so that it can be inspected. If your child is too large for you to lift and carry easily, this request can be a real problem. Ask for individual inspection instead, in a private area, preferably where your child won't have to be moved out of her chair. Ask for a manager if you're refused, and calmly hold up the line until you're given respectful treatment.

If your child is over two years old or over forty pounds, she will probably not be allowed to sit in your lap, even if she is comfortable there and is not able to sit by herself in an airline seat. Bring a specialized child safety seat for automobiles that meets her needs. It will save your child the possible, unpleasant alternative of being flown on a medical transport stretcher. Ask the airline ahead of time about the dimensions of the seats you will be flying in, to make sure your child's seat will fit.

Once you arrive at your destination, you can rent an accessible van for a price roughly twice that of regular car rental. Two companies that offer airport pickup in major cities in the United States are Wheelers Inc. at (800) 456-1371; and Wheelchair Getaways at (800) 642-2042. You may also be able to arrange van rental through major car rental companies.

FOR MORE INFORMATION:

Exceptional Parent is a support organization for the parents of children with physical, mental, and developmental disabilities. Exceptional Parent can be reached at (800) EPARENT or (201) 489-0871, or by writing to 120 State St., Hackensack, NJ 07601-5421. They will answer your questions, or at least point you in the right direction for finding out more about the resources available to you and your child. Exceptional Parent also publishes an annual resource guide, a book catalog, and a monthly magazine.

The Society for the Advancement of Travel for the Handicapped can provide information on tours and trips for the disabled. Its quarterly newsletter, available to members, gives the latest information on accessibility and destination planning. Contact them at (212) 447-7284, or write to them at 347 Fifth Ave., New York, NY 10016.

Travelin' Talk is a network of people and organizations who are willing to provide travelers with disabilities with information before and during their trips. Travelin' Talk also publishes a quarterly newsletter. P.O. Box 3534, Clarksville, TN 37043 (615) 552-6670.

The Directory of Travel Agencies for the Disabled is a guide that is updated annually, listing over 370 agencies that specialize in travel for the deaf, the blind, and the developmentally and physically disabled. Its listings are primarily for travel in the United States and Canada, but it also offers some international information. The cost is $19.95 plus $3 shipping, available from the Disability Book Shop, Vancouver, WA; (800) 637-2256.

The Directory of Accessible Van Rentals is also available from the Disability Book Shop at (800) 637-2256. Its cost is $9.95 plus $3 shipping.

59. Stress relievers for your children

Travel is stressful for children, for some more than others. The only stress reliever available to very young infants will be a good cry, however emotionally jarring that experience will be

for you. If your infant needs to cry to let off the stress of an unfamiliar environment, let her. Make sure that there is nothing else
bothering her, of course. If she's not hungry, tired, wet, messy,
or in pain, then chances are she's taking advantage of her natural coping mechanism. Be with her, hold her, rock her, comfort
her in all the ways you know best. She will stop eventually.

Take advantage of a diaper-changing time to give your
stressed-out infant or toddler a soothing massage. Put a little oil
in your hand, look her in the eye, and tell her, "I'm going to rub
your leg now." Rub gently, but with enough pressure to engen-
der confidence in your touch and to relax her. Say "I'm going
to rub your other leg now," and do so; then move to the arms,
torso, neck, and head. Concentrate on making your touch
gentle and soothing to your child. You may want to hum her
favorite song while massaging her.

For older children, give them room and freedom to let out
their excess energy as soon as possible after a long trip. Choose
accommodations that have space to play and run safely. Plan
the first day's activities so that they include a lot of fresh air and
exercise whenever possible, and plan to spend time with your
children in a safe, kid-friendly environment where you'll rarely,
if ever, have to say "No!" to them. That could be as simple as a
day by the hotel pool.

"Time Out" is not only a good method for disciplining older
children, but also a good stress reliever for them. Often a few
minutes of quiet time away from the cause of your child's
behavior is all that is needed to calm her down.

And for children of any age, a warm bath is soothing and
familiar. Get into the bath with your children to give them an
extra feeling of safety and comfort—not to mention giving
yourself those same nice feelings.

60. Stress relievers for you

Your most natural reaction to your baby's crying is fight-or-
flight: Your body will tense, you'll release adrenaline into your
bloodstream, your level of anxiety will increase, and you'll want
desperately to rescue your child from whatever is bothering

her. When on vacation, you may also be more impatient than usual, wanting to solve your baby's crying problem quickly so you can get on with having fun.

If your baby is crying inconsolably, try to remind yourself that it is likely to be a coping mechanism for her, and that her crying is a healthy reaction to a new situation when you're away from home. You'll need to fight your natural physiological reactions to her crying with a dose of rational thought.

A natural coping mechanism for mothers is breast-feeding. It will create natural opiates in your bloodstream, calming you as it calms your baby. When traveling with a breast-fed baby, it's best to throw feeding schedules out the window, and to sit down and take the time to be with your baby whenever you or she needs it. Don't fight it. Don't try to cut short feeding times so you can get through your day's itinerary. Take the time for yourself and your baby.

Learn to recognize the stress that your children's crying causes you, and to relieve that stress before it overwhelms you. Simply becoming aware of your breathing is a tremendous help, and takes no time away from your need to comfort your child. Breathe in deeply and slowly through your nose, and breathe out through your mouth. Become aware of the tension in your jaw and your shoulders as you breathe out, and let it go. Breathe in again through your nose, out through your mouth. As you relax your jaw, throat, and shoulders on the exhale, you may even find yourself saying a long, low "Ahhh!" That's a good sound, indicating that you're relaxing and letting go of tension, and it will also comfort your baby as you hold her to your chest.

Older children may also cry, whine, or exhibit other signs of unhappiness such as increased crankiness or misbehavior when in a stressful new situation. They may require increased attention and understanding from you, and they may temporarily sap your energy. Don't let your energy stores go unreplenished. If you're traveling with your spouse, make sure that you are both meeting your commitments to one another, and sharing the load equally. Ask for a break when you need it. Go for a walk or a five-minute swim in the hotel pool. On days when your kids have been overwhelming, renew one another's energy with a gentle but strong shoulder, head, or foot massage. Above all, don't let a bad moment become a bad day, and don't let a bad day become a bad week: Take time to put each experience in perspective and to learn from it, so that next time it's easier to cope.

Chapter 10

Emergency! How to Prevent Them—and What to Do If You Can't

Maybe we all have fond memories of the risks we took on vacations when we were single and carefree—stuff that will curl our hair if our own kids ever come home and say they've tried. But now that you're a parent, the choices you make and the risks you take while on vacation don't only affect you, but also your children. That means that a certain level of alertness and prudence is in order. This chapter isn't meant to paralyze you with fear, but rather to give you the best chance of avoiding emergencies in your travels altogether: The best emergency is the one that doesn't happen.

As soon as you get to your destination, prepare yourself and your family for every emergency by getting the local emergency numbers, particularly if you're in an area not serviced by 911. Write down and keep handy numbers for the local emergency department, ambulance services, poison control center, fire-fighting services, and police, along with the number of your doctor at home as well as a local pediatrician, if you've received a referral.

61. We were robbed!

If you are robbed, offer no resistance. Let go of your purse or wallet. Make no attempt to scrutinize your assailant. Get yourself and your children to safety as soon as possible.

Most travel theft, however, will be nonconfrontational. You're jostled while in line for a taxi, or distracted while checking in at your hotel. You may not even realize you've been robbed until hours later when you reach for your wallet and it isn't there.

In either case, get your children to a safe place, and give them as much comfort as they need. Remember that you'll be frightened or tense, and these feelings will come through loud and clear to your child. You will need to file a police report if you plan to file insurance claims later, but worry about these details only after you're sure your children no longer need your undivided attention.

The best response to being robbed is to be prepared before it happens. Here is a checklist:

1. Take traveler's checks for your cash needs. Clean out your wallet and take along only the credit cards you'll use.
2. Leave with a friend your traveler's check numbers, your credit card numbers, and a list of phone numbers to call in the event that any of these are stolen on your trip. If you travel frequently and/or use many cards, join a credit card registry through one of your card memberships, which gives you one number to call to cancel all your cards.
3. Don't call attention to yourself with fancy luggage or other obvious signs of wealth.
4. Carry passports, driver's licenses, and other ID separately from money and traveler's checks.
5. Don't accept any room that doesn't have deadbolts and a peephole.
6. Leave all valuables in the hotel safe, never in your room. Even in hotels with electronic key systems, dozens of people will have keys to your room, and theft is extremely hard to prove. Get a detailed receipt from hotel staff before leaving items in their safe.

7. Thieves know you'll let go of possessions quickly to safeguard your children, so make your possessions less obvious. Whenever possible, wear your camera and purse straps under a coat or sweater. Opt for a money belt instead of a purse or wallet.

8. Always know where you're going and how to get there. If you do get lost, ask a police officer, store owners, or mail carriers for help, not just anyone hanging around.

9. Remember that kids' legs aren't very long, so fleeing an assailant won't be a viable option. Protect yourself by staying in well-lighted, well-populated areas.

62. We were car-jacked!

If you are accosted while getting into or out of a parked car, the most important thing for you to focus on is getting your children to safety. You may need to buy time to physically get them out of their car seats. Do not plead or otherwise negotiate with your assailant for that time, however. Instead, get out of the car and drop or throw the keys and your purse or wallet to the ground, offering no resistance. Get the kids while your assailant gets the keys. Leave everything else and walk away.

The best response to car-jacking is to never be in that situation, of course. Here's how to avoid it:

1. You've just arrived after a long plane ride, you're tired and hot, and now you have to get your kids, your luggage, and yourself to the hotel. It's an easy time to get lost and to end up in a dangerous part of town. Treat yourself, and take a taxi from the airport. Rent your car at your hotel, after you have the chance to ask the hotel staff about potentially dangerous neighborhoods in the area.

2. Request a car that has no logos, stickers, license plate designation, or other outward signs that it is a rental car. Make sure that you can lock both the windows and the doors from the driver's seat.

3. If your budget allows it and you're visiting a high-crime city, rent a cellular phone along with the car, for use in emergencies. Daily charges are usually under

$5, plus a separate toll charge for each call—a good buy for a quick call to the police when you need it.

4. Always know where you're going and how to get there. If you're sitting at the curb with the engine idling and a map on your lap, you're a prime target.

5. Park in well-lit, busy, and secure areas. Have your keys in hand as you approach the car. Check around, under, and inside the car before you unlock it and get in.

6. Some car-jackers gain access to your car by staging minor accidents. If you are hit by another car in an isolated area, then drive slowly to a well-lit, busy place before getting out. Put on your flashers to signal to the other driver that you are doing so.

7. Keep your car in gear when stopped at a light, keep your doors locked, and be prepared to drive away the moment you feel threatened.

63. My child is lost!

Be prepared to do the following if your active child somehow slips out of your sight:

1. Yell "I can't find my child!" to alert adults in the area, and call your child by name. If there are others there to help you, they will. Enlist their help with a brief description of your child: sex, age, and what she's wearing.

2. Don't forget your other children—make sure they are in safe hands before you run off in a panic.

3. Ask yourself when you saw your child last, how far she could have traveled on her own steam, and which directions would be the most dangerous for her, given her probable distance away from where you are now. Search in the most life-threatening direction first: for example, first in the direction of the pool, then the street.

4. Check the exits, then work backward. After you've searched any areas that pose immediate dangers, search towards the nearest exit, to minimize the risk of her leaving the immediate area. Ask others to help you make sure your child doesn't leave an area before she is found.

5. Don't be embarrassed by making noise, calling out loudly and frequently to your child, asking for help from everyone in sight, and using every other available means to find her quickly, including public address systems that will alert others to your child being lost, or calling 911 or other local emergency numbers for assistance as soon as you've determined that she's not in the immediate vicinity.

To avoid that sick feeling in the pit of your stomach when you've lost sight of your child, try to make sure it never happens. Have one adult whose sole responsibility is to look after the children when you're out. That's all she does. It's simply not possible to do anything else, even so much as look at a price tag—and not risk having your active, curious, more-quick-than-you-ever-could-imagine child get away from you and into danger.

If you're traveling with a friend who has children of her own, take turns watching the children for each other, rather than each of you trying to keep track of your own child while you're also trying to do other things. Trade the child-watching responsibility as frequently as you need to, to keep one another fresh and alert and enjoying yourselves.

Another way of keeping track of your child while in an unfamiliar area is a containment strategy: carrying your child on your body in a pack or sling, strapping her into a stroller with a childproof belt, or using a safety harness. Don't plan to travel with your children unless you have either an adult in your party assigned to watch them at all times, or a way of keeping them close to you if you're out with them on your own.

64. My child is sick!

When do you call a doctor, and when do you rely on your children's natural resources and your own nurturing skills to help your children through an illness? Every parent will have a different answer. Some parents will call their child's pediatrician at the first sign of a fever or a cold or a rash; others never see or speak with their pediatrician except for an occasional well-baby visit. For common childhood ailments, trust your instincts about what's best for your children.

When you're on vacation, there's no reason to change your attitude about how to manage your child's health. Try instead to duplicate the level of medical support that makes you most comfortable when you're at home. If you like consulting with your doctor, or your child has frequent ailments that need medical attention, then ask your doctor for a referral at your destination. If you are a member of a health maintenance organization (HMO) or a nationwide clinical network, a referral should be especially convenient to arrange.

If your children are prone to childhood ailments, choose a vacation where a child's cold won't be catastrophic to your plans. Stay put instead of traveling around, and choose a spot where you'll have fun even if you need to curtail some of your activities until your child is on the mend.

If you need professional medical help, first call the doctor you've been referred to; if she's not available ask for the on-call physician and explain the problem. If you don't have a doctor, ask the front desk of your hotel if there is a doctor on call, or if they can refer you. Consult the phone book as a last resort. Don't go to a hospital emergency room for medical aid unless you have an emergency. Although you'll be treated eventually, life-threatening cases will take precedence, and you'll be subjecting your child to a long wait.

FOR MORE INFORMATION:

Doctors By Phone is a medical advice hotline that operates seven days a week in all fifty states between 8 A.M. and midnight, Eastern time. (900) 77-DOCTOR ($3 a minute).

Ask-A-Nurse is a twenty-four-hour service that puts you in touch with a nurse in certain states. (800) 535-1111.

65. My child is hurt!—An emergency medical guide

Before you go or as soon as you arrive, be prepared for emergencies by looking up emergency numbers for the local police, fire, ambulance, poison center, and ambulance services. Keep these numbers with you at all times, along with the number of a local pediatrician if you've received one from your doctor at home.

The following information is printed courtesy of the American Academy of Pediatrics. It should not be used as a substitute for the medical care and advice of your pediatrician. There may be variations in treatment that your pediatrician may recommend based on the individual facts and circumstances. They are also not meant to substitute for direct CPR training and first-aid classes, which should be high on the list of priorities for every parent with small children.

First Aid

BURNS AND SCALDS

Minor Burns Without Blisters

Place burned extremity into cold water or cover burned part with a towel soaked in cold water until the pain stops (at least 15 minutes). Do not use ice.

Burns With Blisters

Same as above; do **NOT** break the blisters. Call your doctor for advice on how to cover the burn. ANY burn on the face, hands, feet, or genitals and any large burn should be seen by a doctor.

Large or Deep Burns

Call 911 or an emergency ambulance. Remove clothing. Do **NOT** apply any medication. Keep child warm with a clean sheet and then a blanket until help arrives.

Chemical Burns (See "Poisons: Skin Exposure"), **Electrical Burns**
Disconnect electrical power. Do **NOT** touch victim with bare hands. Pull victim away from power source with wood or a thick, dry cloth. ALL electrical burns need to be seen by a doctor.

CONVULSIONS (SEIZURES)

Protect the child from injury. Perform rescue breathing if child is blue or not breathing. If breathing, lay child on side. Put nothing in the mouth. Call 911 or an emergency ambulance.

EYE INJURIES

If anything is splashed in the eye, flush gently with water for at least 15 minutes. Call the Poison Center or doctor for further advice. Any injured or painful eye should be seen by a doctor. Do **NOT** touch or rub the injured eye. Do **NOT** apply medication. Do **NOT** remove objects stuck into the eye. Gently bandage the painful eye shut until you can get medical help.

FAINTING

Lay child on back with head to the side and legs raised. Do **NOT** give anything by mouth. Call your doctor. If child does not wake up right away, call 911 or an emergency ambulance.

FEVER

A child who feels hot to the touch, complains of being hot, or is sweating or chilling may have a fever. Take child's temperature. Give fever medication as recommended by your doctor to reduce fever. Do not sponge a child with ice or alcohol. If the child is hot from sun exposure or exercise, get child to cooler, shaded area to rest; give lots of fluids. Whatever you suspect the cause of fever may be, call your doctor. This is especially important for babies less than three months of age.

FRACTURES AND SPRAINS

DO **NOT** MOVE A CHILD WHO MAY HAVE A BACK OR NECK INJURY, because this may cause serious harm. If an injured part is painful, swollen, deformed, or if motion causes pain, suspect a fracture and splint it. Apply a cold compress and call your doctor or an ambulance.

HEAD INJURIES

DO **NOT** MOVE ANY CHILD WHO MAY HAVE A SERIOUS HEAD AND/OR NECK OR BACK INJURY, because this may cause harm.
Call 911 or an emergency ambulance for any of the following:

- Any loss of consciousness or drowsiness
- Persistent headache or vomiting
- Clumsiness or inability to move any body part
- Oozing blood or watery fluid from ears or nose
- Convulsions (seizures)
- Abnormal speech or behavior

For questions about less serious injuries, call your doctor.

NOSEBLEEDS

With child sitting, squeeze nostrils together between your thumb and index finger for 10 minutes. If bleeding persists, call your doctor.

POISONS

If a child is unconscious, becoming drowsy, having convulsions, or having trouble breathing, call 911 or an emergency ambulance.

Swallowed Poisons

Any nonfood substance is a potential poison. Call the Poison Center immediately. Do not induce vomiting except on professional advice. The Poison Center will give you further instructions.

Fumes, Gases, or Smoke

Get the victim into fresh air. Call 911 or fire department. If the child is not breathing, start CPR and continue until help arrives.

Skin Exposure

If acids, lye, pesticides, chemicals, or any potentially poisonous substances come in contact with a child's skin, gently brush off dry material. Remove contaminated clothing. Wear rubber gloves if possible. Wash skin with large quantities of soap and water. Call Poison Center for further advice.

SKIN WOUNDS

For all of these conditions, make sure your child is properly immunized for tetanus.

Bruises

Apply cold compresses for one-half hour. For extensive bruises, crushing injuries, or bicycle spoke injuries, call your doctor. For continued pain or swelling, call your doctor.

Cuts

Apply pressure with a clean cloth to stop the bleeding. If the cut is large and deep, call for help and maintain pressure until help arrives. For minor cuts, wash with soap and water and cover with dressing. If a cut may need stitches, seek medical care as soon as possible.

Scrapes

Wash scrapes with soap and water. Cover with a nonstick dressing.

Splinters

Wash with soap and water. Do not soak splinter. Remove small splinters with tweezers. If not easily removed, call your doctor.

Puncture Wounds

Do **NOT** remove large objects such as knives or sticks. Call your doctor. For minor puncture wounds, wash with soap and water and call your doctor. Your child may need a tetanus booster.

STINGS AND BITES

Stinging Insects

Remove the stinger with the scraping motion of a fingernail. Do **NOT** pull the stinger out. Put a cold compress on the bite to relieve pain. If hives, paleness, weakness, nausea, vomiting, tightness in the chest, breathing difficulty, or collapse occur, call 911 or an emergency ambulance. For spider bites, call your doctor or Poison Center.

Animal or Human Bites

Wash wound thoroughly with soap and water. Call your doctor.

Ticks

Place tweezers close to the head of the tick and pull tick away from point of attachment. Call your doctor if head remains attached, or if child later develops symptoms such as headache, fever or rash.

Snake Bites

Keep child at rest. Call the Poison Center. Do not apply ice. Take the child to an emergency department. Loosely splint injured extremity. Keep extremity at rest, positioned at, or slightly below, the level of the heart.

TEETH

Baby (Primary) Teeth

If knocked out or broken, apply clean gauze to control bleeding and call a dentist.

Permanent Teeth

If knocked out, find the tooth and rinse it gently without touching the root. Insert and gently hold the tooth in its socket or transport the tooth in cow's milk. Go directly to the dentist or an emergency department. Time is important.

If broken, save the pieces. Gently clean the injured area with warm water. Place a cold compress to reduce swelling. Go to the dentist immediately.

Choking/CPR

FOR INFANTS UNDER ONE YEAR

CHOKING

Begin the following if the infant is choking and unable to breathe. However, if the infant is coughing, crying, or speaking, DO NOT do any of the following, but call your doctor for further advice.

1. Position infant face down on your arm supporting the head.
2. Give up to 5 back blows with the heel of hand between infant's shoulder blades.

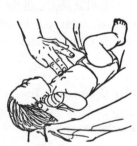

3. Position infant face up on your forearm.
4. Give up to 5 chest thrusts near center of breastbone.

Repeat steps 1 to 4 until object is coughed up or infant starts to breathe or becomes unconscious. If infant becomes unconscious:

5. Lift jaw and tongue. If foreign object is seen, sweep it out with finger.
6. Tilt head back. Try to give 2 breaths.

Go to step 3 on p. 117, "Cardiopulmonary Resuscitation."

FOR INFANTS UNDER ONE YEAR
CARDIOPULMONARY RESUSCITATION

To be used when infant is unresponsive or when breathing or heart beat stops.

1. Tilt head back. Seal your lips tightly around infant's mouth and nose.

2. Give 2 slow breaths until chest gently rises.

If air goes in:
3. Briefly check for a pulse.

If there's a pulse:
4. Give 1 slow breath every three seconds for about 1 minute (20 breaths).
5. Recheck pulse about every minute.

Continue rescue breathing as long as pulse is present but infant is not breathing.

If no pulse:
4. Find finger position near center of breastbone.
5. Compress chest 5 times.
6. Give 1 slow breath.
7. Repeat cycles of 5 compressions to 1 breath until you feel a pulse or help arrives.

If air won't go in:
3. Retilt head back. Try to give 2 breaths again.

4. Position infant face down on your arm, supporting the head.
5. Give up to 5 back blows with the heel of hand between infant's shoulder blades.

6. Position infant face up on your forearm.
7. Give up to 5 chest thrusts near center of breastbone.
8. Lift jaw and tongue. If foreign object is seen, sweep it out with finger.

Repeat steps 3 to 8 until breaths go in or infant starts to breathe on own.

Choking/CPR

FOR CHILDREN OVER ONE YEAR

CHOKING

Begin the following if the child is choking and unable to breathe. However, if the child is coughing, crying, or speaking, DO NOT do any of the following, but call your doctor for further advice.

1. Place thumbside of fist against middle of abdomen just above the navel. Grasp fist with the other hand.
2. Give up to 5 quick upper thrusts.

Repeat steps 1 to 2 until object is coughed up or child starts to breathe or becomes unconscious.

FOR CHILDREN OVER ONE YEAR
CARDIOPULMONARY RESUSCITATION

To be used when child is unresponsive or when breathing or heart beat stops.
1. Tilt head back. Seal your lips tightly around child's mouth and nose; pinch nose shut.
2. Give 2 slow breaths until chest gently rises.

If air goes in:
3. Briefly check for a pulse.

If there's a pulse:

4. Give 1 slow breath every 3 seconds for about 1 minute (20 breaths).
5. Recheck pulse about every minute.

Continue rescue breathing as long as pulse is present but child is not breathing.

If no pulse:
4. Find hand position near center of breastbone.
5. Position shoulders over hands
6. Compress chest 5 times.
7. Give 1 slow breath.
8. Repeat cycles of 5 compressions to 1 breath until you feel a pulse or help arrives.

If air won't go in:
3. Retilt head back. Try to give 2 breaths again.

4. Place heel of 1 hand on child's abdomen above middle of navel and below rib cage.
5. Give up to 5 abdominal thrusts.

6. Lift jaw and tongue. If foreign object is seen, sweep it out with finger.

Repeat steps 3 to 6 until breaths go in or child starts to breathe on own.

66. Medical supplies to bring along

Don't try to be a paramedic, especially if you're traveling by air (you'll want to keep your luggage to a mini
mum) or to a place where you'll be able to buy medical supplies on an as-needed basis. A good rule is to leave it out of your suitcase, unless you know already that you'll need it, or you know that if you do need it, you won't want to make your child wait while you go to the store. Here's a recommended list:

1. **Prescriptions and allergy medicines.** Remember that pharmacists in some states may not take a nonlocal prescription. Have your pharmacist's and your pediatrician's numbers handy in case you need to replace lost medicine. Don't forget to take along eyeglass prescriptions, too.
2. **Sunscreen.** SPF 15 or higher, for use on children six months or older.
3. **Diaper rash ointment.** Choose one that is zinc oxide–based, so it can be alternatively used as a sunscreen on noses and ears. It's especially useful for children under six months, who are too young to use regular sunscreen.
4. **Sterile bandages and antibiotic ointment.** For cuts and scrapes, if your child is mobile.
5. **Optional medicines: children's acetaminophen**, if your child is prone to fever; **syrup of ipecac**, to induce vomiting in the event that your child swallows a noncaustic, poisonous substance; an **electrolyte replacement solution** especially made for children with diarrhea such as Pedialyte or Infalyte, and **fiber tablets or powder**, which are useful for both constipation and diarrhea. Ask your pediatrician for dosage recommendations before you travel.

   If you're camping or hiking, you need to balance your increased need for self-sufficiency with your need to carry everything yourself. When the Wilderness Medical Society conducted a recent poll in Yosemite National Park, it discovered that 14 percent of hikers polled had been forced to cut their trip short because of an easily treatable injury, such as blistered feet or sunburn. So it does pay to take some supplies along. Take into consideration the length of your planned trip as well as any unique risks in the environment where you'll be traveling.

In addition to the above medical supply recommendations, include these in your backpack:

6. **Small scissors and moleskin.** Or other foot protection that you can cut to fit your feet or your children's, and that offers relief from and protection against blisters.
7. **Calamine lotion.** For insect bites or sunburn.
8. **A thermometer.** To gauge how sick your child is and whether you need to cut your trip short.
9. **Tweezers.** To remove ticks and/or splinters.

A number of companies market first-aid kits for traveling families. You'll find these advertised in any outdoor magazine or travel magazine. If you decide to order one, be sure to tell them the ages of your children so that they send an age-appropriate kit.

67. Playing it safe when traveling solo with your kids

When you are solely responsible for your children's health and welfare, you need to be more cautious. Here are some suggestions:

1. Remember that the cardinal rule in a bad situation— to run away from it—will be difficult with little children. Be especially cautious about traveling at night or in sparsely populated areas.
2. If you are driving, decide ahead of time where you'll stop for the night, and make reservations. Plan to arrive well before dark.
3. Book hotels that offer round-the-clock assistance and check-in, as well as an on-site restaurant.
4. Ask a hotel employee to escort you and your children to your room. Keep your doors and windows locked

unless they are inaccessible from the outside. Make
sure the room has deadbolts and a peephole, and don't
open the door unless you recognize who is there. If it
is a hotel staffperson, ask to see identification before
opening the door.

5. Take-out food is a great boon after a long day with your
kids. Have the food delivered to the front desk, though,
and if your kids are too rambunctious to take with you
down to the front desk, ask the hotel staff to bring the
food up to you. Or use the hotel room service.

6. Know where you're going before you leave the hotel,
and ask hotel staff for any particular safety precautions. If you're driving, use valet parking or ask for an
escort to your car.

68. Insurance needs for traveling families

As you add children to your family, you're also adding to the
number of variables that might go wrong while you're on vacation. What if your baby gets too sick to travel and you've
already paid up-front for that expensive cruise package? What
if your older child finds out the hard way on your vacation that
she's allergic to bee stings, requiring emergency medical attention while away from home? What if your bags all get lost in
transit—a mere inconvenience for adults, but an absolute dis-
aster when your kids are with you? You'll avoid making a bad
situation worse if you have insurance.

Don't go overboard on insurance coverage, of course. Make
sure you're getting value that's more or less in line with what
you're paying for the insurance. And above all, know where
you're already covered, to avoid costly duplication. Here's a
look at how to evaluate your insurance options:

Medical insurance. If your children have an accident or
become sick while you're vacationing, you don't want to
second-guess your medical insurance coverage. Before
you buy additional insurance specifically for your trip,
know what your existing insurance covers. Members of

you buy additional insurance specifically for your trip, know what your existing insurance covers. Members of Health Maintenance Organizations (HMOs), in particular, should fully understand how their HMO will cover medical expenses if a member needs to use medical facilities that are not a part of the HMO. Some HMOs will stipulate that you must use their clinics if there is one within twenty miles of where a medical emergency takes place. Others will honor bills from nonmember clinics, if the bills were incurred while a family was away from home. Ask them, before you need to know the answers.

In addition to your health insurance, your credit cards may offer you substantial coverage for travel-related accidents and illnesses. Some card companies will also pay for medical evacuation from international destinations, something that your standard health insurance policy will rarely cover. Check with each of your card companies. Since card membership is usually far less expensive than a new medical insurance policy will be, you may also want to call competing card companies to see who has the best travel-related services, and to order new cards from the companies that meet your needs.

If you're unhappy with the amount of coverage your current medical policies give you for travel-related illnesses and accidents, then look into a one-time travel insurance policy that will cover physician, hospital, and emergency transport fees. You'll more likely need additional coverage if you're planning an extended international trip. Like any insurance negotiation, you'll need to ask about deductibles, the coverage of preexisting medical conditions, copayment policies, and methods for reimbursement.

Auto insurance. You probably already have insurance that covers your rental car on your own automobile policy. Check the fine print before you go, so you won't have to try to second-guess your coverage while standing in front of the car rental counter, crying children in hand and a line of customers behind you. Remember that you'll be driving in an unfamiliar place and in an unfamiliar car: You may want to boost the amount of rental-car coverage you have on your own policy. Paying by some credit cards will also give you additional collision protection, although card companies will rarely cover medical liability. Again, check before you get to the rental counter.

Trip cancellation insurance. Trip cancellation insurance reimburses you for the cost of prepaid travel that is canceled or interrupted by an emergency. It provides no medical coverage in the case of illness or hospitalization. So it makes sense only if you've made a significant, nonrefundable investment in your vacation.

It's certainly a possibility, when you have children, that something will come up that prevents you from traveling when you plan to. But most trip cancellation insurance policies are very strict about when they'll reimburse you. Make sure that the cancellation policy covers what you consider are the likely reasons that you'll need to cancel. Some policies will insure against cancellation for any reason. But these policies are available only with very high deductibles.

Theft/Lost-baggage insurance. The best lost-baggage insurance is to carry what you need on the plane with you. But keep in mind that your homeowner's insurance will likely cover much of your loss, even if a theft occurs while you're away from home. Check your existing coverage, and add to it only when you understand what you're covered for already. If you do decide to purchase additional coverage, make sure you understand whether what you are paying for covers the depreciated value or the replacement value.

FOR MORE INFORMATION:

Access America (800) 284-8300, **USAssist** (800) 225-5911, **International SOS Assistance** (800) 225-5911, **Mutual of**

Omaha (800) 228-9792, **Travel Assistance International** (800) 821-2828, **Travel Guard International** (800) 826-1300, **Health Care Abroad** (800) 237-6615, and **Travmed** (800) 732-5309, all provide one-time medical coverage insurance for travelers. Some additionally offer insurance for baggage loss, trip cancellation, or trip interruption. Your travel agent may have recommendations of her own. Don't buy an insurance package that covers more than you need, and shop around until you're satisfied.

Chapter 11
Take a Break: Finding a Good Baby-sitter When You Need One

It may be hard to imagine wanting to spend time away from your children while on vacation, especially if you work outside the home and never see enough of them as it is. But a little time for yourself or with your spouse can be wonderful. You'll return to your children refreshed and relaxed, with your energy stores recharged.

69. Finding good child care while on vacation

If you are staying at a large hotel in the United States, the concierge will most likely have a list of licensed, bonded, insured baby-sitting services in the immediate area if they don't provide child care on-site. But most hotels will just hand you a list. They won't usually give you recommendations, per se, since that could leave them open to liability lawsuits. So you'll be on your own when it comes to choosing the right caregiver for your children.

If your hotel doesn't even provide a list of possible care-givers, or if you're renting a condominium or private home, you can call Child Care Aware, a national service for quality child-care referrals, at (800) 424-2246. Child Care Aware will be able to refer you to the local clearinghouse number for licensed child-care providers at your destination, which will give you a far greater number of choices than a hotel list. Once you call the local referral service, be sure to ask for caregivers that provide, or better yet, that specialize in short-term care.

Your choices may include both baby-sitters who will come to the hotel, and centers that offer drop-in care. Baby-sitters offer convenience, but are usually less experienced than caregivers at day-care centers. A baby-sitter will usually come to stay with your child in your hotel room, not usually a very interesting place for kids.

Drop-in child-care facilities are less convenient (you'll usually have to drive there), but will be better equipped and usually staffed with more experienced people. Some sites specialize in drop-in care exclusively, and may even offer a complementary beeper service, so that you can stay in touch with your children at all times.

Start your evaluation of caregivers with these questions over the telephone:

1. Is the caregiver licensed, bonded, and insured?
2. How long have they been in business? Remember that some established businesses may have been taken over recently by a new owner. Ask about the current owner's track record.
3. What is the level of experience among caregivers? This is your most critical question. Look for a minimum of two years' experience working with small children, some course work in child development, and mandatory, up-to-date training in CPR for infants and children as well as other first-aid skills.
4. What is the caregiver's philosophy about disciplining children? Asking such an open-ended question will give you a sense of the caregiver's style, and whether you feel comfortable with it.

Once you choose a caregiver over the telephone, here are some additional questions to ask yourself once you meet in person:

1. Does she treat your children like human beings? Does she seem to like your children, and they her? Does she get down on their level to speak with them?
2. If you've taken your children to a drop-in care center instead of meeting the caregiver in your hotel, is the area bright, pleasant, and safe? Do the other children there seem to be happy?
3. Does the caregiver give you a comfortable feeling? Trust your instincts, and your children's. If you don't feel good about this person, then don't leave your children with her. Say instead, "I'm sorry. I don't think this arrangement will work, and thank you for your time."

To avoid feeling embarrassed about changing your mind, or feeling that you have to go through with a bad commitment, make sure that you establish in your first telephone conversation, before you meet, that either party is free to change their minds if the situation doesn't feel right.

70. How to evaluate child care at all-inclusive resorts (before they take your money)

Resorts may claim to do it all, but sometimes they *don't*. Young children are the least likely guests to complain about the service, especially those children who haven't yet learned to talk. So unfortunately, while a given resort might offer lavish accommodations, gourmet food on demand, and wildly exciting activities for adults, their littlest guests might get short shrift. Finding that out ahead of time takes more work than looking through the resort's glossy brochures.

Note that many resorts will not offer licensed care—they don't need to in many states, since the parents are assumed to be on-site. And of course if your destination is international, you can't count on anything at all. In these circumstances, beyond doing your mandatory fact-checking about the experience level and safety training of the personnel, you need to do more.

Your best bet is to take the recommendations of friends and acquaintances who have personal experience with the child care of a given resort. Make sure, though, that your children are going to be in the same age group; some resorts do two- to-four-year-olds very well, but have abysmal facilities for infants.

After friends, you can also rely on a reputable family travel agent. Make sure that the agent can personally vouch for the child-care services of the place she is booking for you.

Another indicator of quality is to consider how many years a given resort has been in business, and how long they've offered family programs. Usually a poorly-run child-care facility is the kiss of death for any family resort, so if a facility has been in business for ten years or longer, it's a good indication that their child-care programs are working.

Once you narrow in on a potential list of resorts, try to interview the director of the child-care programs before you make your final choice. Ask about the experience level of the staff (they should have at least two years of experience working with small children); the ratio of caregivers to children (this should not exceed 4:1 for the infant program; or 6:1 for children over three years); and whether all members of the staff have had first-aid and CPR training.

71. Should you bring your baby-sitter along?

Let's say you have a favorite baby-sitter—a neighborhood teenager or grandmother who is reliable and beloved by your children. What better way to solve the child-care problem than to bring that baby-sitter along?

Think again. Unless you have a full-time nanny or au pair for your children and have already worked out a detailed contractual arrangement with your employee, you are going to be treading on some very murky ground when it comes to fair employment practices, minimum wage laws, tax withholding, and liability in the event of an accident or health crisis. A simple arrangement of free room-and-board in exchange for baby-sitting a few hours a day can soon become a complicated morass of unpleasant misunderstandings between you and your baby-sitter.

But bringing a caregiver along is still an excellent idea. The trick is to choose traveling companions who will want to be with your children for their own company, not because you pay them to be. How? Either by opting for intergenerational travel with your parents, or by traveling with a family with whom you are already close, whose children you also enjoy. Adding more adults to the travel mix gives you more freedom to pursue activities on your vacation that don't include your children—while knowing that they are with responsible adults whom your children already know well.

72. Preparing your children to be without you for a while

Preparing your children to be without you while on vacation takes a little more time and thought than if you were merely arranging for a baby-sitter to come to your home while you go out for the evening. Remember that you've already changed your children's environment by taking them to a new place. Be respectful of the stress such a change may cause your children, when asking them to also get used to a new caregiver for a few hours. Here are some tips for making the experience a smooth and happy one for your kids:

1. Don't plan to be away from your children for the first few days after arriving at a new place. They'll need you close by to give them a sense of continuity and comfort.

2. If they are old enough, talk to your children ahead of time about your plans to leave them with a caregiver for a while. Let them know how long you will be gone, and when you will be coming back. Give your children plenty of opportunity to discuss thoroughly with you any misgivings they might have.

3. Once they're ready to be left with a caregiver, don't sneak out without saying good-bye. Give them a hug and tell them when you'll be seeing them again, even if you think that they're too young to understand.

Developmental experts believe that even very young infants will respond and be comforted by you taking time to say good-bye, and that they may feel anxious and betrayed if you instead simply disappear for a while.

FOR MORE INFORMATION:

Child Care Aware is a nonprofit organization founded in 1988 to improve the quality and consistency of child-care programs in the United States. The organization provides a Parent Hotline, (800) 424-2246, which will provide at no cost the name and telephone number of a child-care resource and referral agency in the community where you plan to travel. Child Care Aware will also provide at no cost a brochure on choosing quality child care and a take-along checklist for interviewing potential child-care providers.

The National Association for the Education of Young Children (NAEYC) runs a nationwide certification program that assures a high and consistent level of quality of care across the United States. NAEYC-accredited child-care programs won't always provide drop-in care, but it's worth asking about. The NAEYC recommends that you go through the local child-care resource and referral agency, whose number will be provided to you by Child Care Aware, above. Ask the agency if they're aware of NAEYC-accredited programs that offer drop-in care.

You can call the NAEYC directly to ask for their brochures, "Developmentally Appropriate Practices in Early Childhood Programs Serving Infants," "Developmentally Appropriate Practices in Early Childhood Programs Serving Toddlers," "Developmentally Appropriate Practice in Early Childhood Programs Serving Younger Preschoolers," and "Good Teaching Practices for Older Preschoolers and Kindergartners," each available for fifty cents. These brochures give extremely detailed recommendations for interactions between caregivers and children at each age, and will give you additional clues for what to look for when choosing a caregiver for your children while on vacation. The NAEYC is located at 1509 16th St. NW, Washington, DC, 20036-1426. Or call them at (800) 424-2460.

Chapter 12
The Great Outdoors

Many vacations involve being outdoors, whether it's by the pool, on the beach, in a national park, or simply walking from place to place. Active vacations are a natural with young children, with their inexhaustible stores of energy. A few simple health precautions and a good understanding of your child's developmental needs are all you need to make your outdoor vacation fun for everyone.

73. Sun strategies

The skin of blond or red-headed babies is especially vulnerable to burns, but all young babies, no matter what their natural skin tone, need to be protected, since babies have thinner, more sensitive skin and will burn more easily than an adult will with the same skin tone. Remember, too, that it doesn't have to be hot—the sun burns just as effectively when it's cold outside, and reflective glare from snow can increase your children's chances of getting burned. It doesn't even have to be sunny: Ultraviolet (UV) radiation can penetrate clouds.

The best rule is to eliminate direct sun exposure between 10 A.M. and 2 P.M., and to protect your children with long sleeves, hats, and umbrellas at other times. Zinc oxide can be used even on infants (it's the main ingredient in many diaper-rash ointments), but needs to be put on thickly enough to form a visible barrier, making it impractical for more than your child's nose and ears.

Before six months of age, don't use sunscreen other than zinc oxide unless your doctor recommends it. Some experts believe that exposure before six months can increase the chance of your child developing allergies. After six months, buy sunscreen especially made for children, with a sun protection factor (SPF) of at least 15. Make sure that the sunscreen you choose blocks both UVA and UVB rays. Test the sunscreen on a small patch of your child's skin for allergic reaction before using it everywhere. Sunscreen will take about thirty minutes after application to become effective. Reapply it frequently— even "waterproof" sunblock will be rubbed or toweled off quickly.

Try to keep your children from putting their hands in their mouths after you've put sunscreen on them, and avoid putting it on your children's foreheads, since it will sting if it gets into their eyes. Choose a wide-brimmed hat instead to protect their forehead and face. Depending on your child, you may need to persevere to find a hat that will stay on when she's intent on grabbing what's on top of her head. If she is very insistent, sew a strap onto the hat that has a buckle and adjustable loop, like those found in high-chair safety straps or on shopping carts. You'll be able to adjust this type of strap comfortably but snugly enough to stay on your child's head. Or carry an umbrella with you along with your baby to give her a portable place in the shade.

If you're planning a beach vacation, take along a portable crib, tent, or playpen that offers good shade protection to give your children a safe, cool place to nap out of the sun. There are a number of models on the market, available at any retail baby supply store.

FOR MORE INFORMATION:

The American Cancer Society at (800) ACS-2345 can give you information on how to protect children's skin from the sun. Ask for their free brochure.

The Skin Cancer Foundation monitors sunscreen products. Products that meet the foundation's stringent standards are given a seal of recommendation. For a list of those products send a self-addressed, stamped envelope to The Skin Cancer Foundation, P.O. Box 561, New York, NY 10156.

After the Stork manufactures lightweight, sun-protective clothing. The company claims that their jackets, pants, shorts, and shirts provide twice the sun protection of regular cotton fabric, blocking 99 percent of UVB rays. A product catalog can be ordered by calling (800) 441-4775.

74. Water—the Sirens' call

Water of all kinds—moving or still, chlorinated or natural—may top the list of fascinating attractions for kids. That makes vacations in, on, or near water a favorite for families. But you need to temper that natural enthusiasm for water with your own good sense. Always remember that your kids are too young to understand that the water can kill them.

Drowning is now the nation's third leading cause of accidental death in children under the age of five, just behind automobile accidents and household poisonings. Young children must be watched around water at all times. That means having an adult guardian for each of your children when they play around water.

When boating, canoeing, or just near natural waterways, plan to invest in a Coast Guard–approved personal flotation device for each of your children. Wear one yourself, too, as a good example. Flotation devices are available for even the smallest of infants, and are designed to keep your child face-up in the event of an accident. Choose a neon-colored flotation device and dress your children in brightly colored clothing to make them easy to spot in the water.

Remember that mountain lakes and streams stay cold even in summertime, and that ocean temperatures will be affected quickly by changes in the weather. Cold water can incapacitate a child in minutes. Young children are especially prone to hypothermia. Keep play in the water limited to brief periods in natural water areas, and keep a close eye on your children for signs of being too cold.

Young children have a natural swallowing reflex that can get them into trouble quickly in water. In rivers and lakes, they may ingest disease-causing organisms if their head goes into the water. In chlorinated pools, although the risk of disease is less, the swallowing reflex may still cause your child to ingest enough water to cause illness. Play it safe by keeping your children's heads completely out of the water until they are old enough for swimming lessons, and can learn how to hold their breath.

75. Pool safety

Because young children become chilled more easily than adults, the pool your children swim in should be heated to about 80 degrees. To avoid chill, young children shouldn't spend more than half an hour in the water at one time.

Make out-of-the-water times fun for your children, too, by playing with them or allowing them to order a pool-side lunch once in a while. Contrary to popular belief, you don't need to make your children wait after eating before they go back into the pool.

It's an unfortunate fact that hotel pools with lifeguards are few and far between: More often then not, hotels attempt to skirt liability issues by not hiring guards and posting SWIM AT YOUR OWN RISK signs instead. Take that responsibility seriously. Take a course in CPR. If you are unable to swim yourself or if you're at all uncomfortable in the water, make sure that you bring a spouse or another responsible adult to help watch your children.

Before you let your children in any pool, inspect it for hazards such as drains with loose grates or poorly marked depth indicators. Don't allow your children to jump or dive into any body of water until you've personally inspected it for safe swimming. And stay within arm's length of your children, or better yet get into the pool with them, even if they've had swimming lessons. Perhaps the best advice is to treat that nice, benign-looking swimming pool with the same respect you would a loaded gun, since it can be just as deadly.

76. Is my child old enough for swimming lessons?

Maybe you're considering enrolling your child in a swim class offered by the resort where you're vacationing. But is she old enough? By now we've probably all seen television shows or photographs of small babies swimming happily under water, even from the moment of birth. We've heard about every child's innate ability to swim. We've heard that the answer to drowning tragedies is early "water-proofing" of our infants. What you've seen and heard seems almost too good to be true.

In fact, it is too good to be true.

Drowning can be a very real result of infant and toddler "water-proofing" programs, especially those that require or encourage submersion of the child's head. Parents may be instructed to blow in the child's face to stimulate an intake of breath and then submerge the child in water, mistakenly believing that the child can be water-proofed, even before that child has any sense of the danger water poses.

But even with the increased popularity of infant and toddler swim programs, childhood drowning accidents haven't declined. They've actually increased. Water-proofing programs themselves may actually lead to more deaths by giving children and their parents a false sense of confidence. Approximately one-fourth of all toddlers in serious pool accidents have already had swimming lessons.

What about your friends' kids, the ones who were swimming at six months? With a little help, infants will indeed float and paddle in a pool. But no child of that age has an understanding of water safety, or of the danger that water poses. Child development experts maintain that below the age of three, a child will forget what she has learned and will have no chance of saving herself in an emergency.

Before the age of three, stick with water-play programs that include at least one adult in the pool with each child. After three, let your child be your guide: Begin lessons only if your child feels ready and confident.

Don't consider any swim program unless it has been certified by the YMCA, American Red Cross, or another reliable group. Find out what guidelines the instructor follows, and avoid any program that includes dropping a child into the water or forcing a child beneath the surface.

Stay near the pool for the entire lesson, which should not last for over half an hour. Take your child out if she exhibits any sign of fear or reluctance to do what the instructor is asking of her. First lessons stay with us a long time. If your child isn't absolutely comfortable and absolutely happy, then she isn't ready for lessons.

77. Planning a family ski vacation

Nearly every ski resort offers family programs. After all, getting you out on the slopes even after you've become a parent is plain good business. But the degree of commitment to children's activities will vary greatly from ski area to ski area. Some ski areas—often not the most glamorous or famous resorts—have made a strong commitment to children of all ages. They've trained their staff and they've invested in programs that reflect that commitment. Other ski areas will hand your child a coloring book when you get there and call that their family program.

To avoid getting trapped in a miserable experience, evaluate your choices by these family-friendly criteria before deciding where to take your family skiing:

1. **Geography.** The lodge should be centrally located, an easy walk to ski runs of your ability level, so that you can check on your children often if you leave them in a day-care facility, or can stay in touch with one another if you and your spouse take turns watching the children while the other skis. The lounge should offer spacious nonsmoking areas. Look also for resorts that offer outdoor areas for children to play in the snow, which are protected from the ski slopes but within easy walking distance of the lodge.
2. **"Child-friendliness."** Ideally, there should be an almost level, well-groomed area reserved for the

youngest skiers, where only children, their parents, and certified ski instructors are allowed. These areas should be equipped with easy, safe lift technology. Ask about what lifts are available for all of the easiest slopes! All too often there isn't a lift at all—your child will be trudging up a hill, and not too happily. Lift operators should make a point of helping beginners with the lift, be it a rope tow or a T-bar, and should slow the lift down or stop it whenever a child needs extra help.

3. **Child-care facilities.** If you are a single parent, or if you and your spouse both plan to ski at the same time, child care is obviously important to you. Look for a 4:1 ratio of children to caregivers for children under three; a 6:1 ratio for children over three. Ask if the facility is licensed, bonded, and insured, and what the qualifications of the staff are (minimum qualifications are CPR training and two years' experience working with young children). Ask if they take reservations: If they operate on a first-come, first-served basis, you may miss out. Ask also if they provide or offer referrals for baby-sitters, in case you need help in the evenings.

Make sure you feel comfortable with the physical layout of the rooms, and with the interactions you see between caregivers and children. Are the rooms bright, clean, and well-stocked with age-appropriate toys? Do the caregivers respect the children, speaking to the children directly instead of with each other? Would you like to stay there, if you were a kid?

Much of your investigation of a resort's child-care facilities can be done before you make your reservation deposit. But the most important things—whether your children feel safe, happy, and enthusiastic about staying there—won't be answered until you get there. Ease the adjustment for your kids by planning to be away for only a few hours on the first day or two.

Remember that this is your children's vacation, too. A few minutes' separation anxiety is normal in a new place, but if your children are genuinely unhappy for longer than that, then child care is not the answer for your family. Plan ahead for this contingency by traveling with a spouse or friend, so that you can each purchase half-day lift tickets and take turns being with your children during the other half of the day.

4. **Family programs.** Depending on your children's age, you'll want to ask about ski school and other organized activities. Is instruction available for children your child's age? How long has the program been offered? What are the qualifications of the instructors? Remember, too, that your child's stamina and interest in skiing is not likely to last a full day. Does the resort offer other outdoor play activities for children, or indoor activities if the weather is too unpleasant?

5. **Incentive discounts for families.** The cost of a family ski vacation will depend not so much on quality, frankly, as on the popularity of a given destination. If you don't care where you ski, you'll have the opportunity to bargain-shop, once you determine that a destination offers all of the things that are important. Look for programs that are free for children under twelve, if a parent buys lift tickets.

6. **Bad weather "insurance."** How are the snow-making facilities? What does the resort or the nearby area offer besides skiing, if it rains, or is too cold, or is otherwise not a good time for the slopes? Remember that your children will have far less tolerance and patience with bad weather than you will. Choose a ski area that offers alternatives if the weather doesn't cooperate.

78. Is my child old enough for skiing lessons?

Skiing down a bunny slope rarely risks your child's life. And ski resort operators also have a vested interest in keeping your child enthusiastic about skiing—after all, your child represents a long-term investment in their future. Ski resorts also usually have state-of-the-art medical emergency equipment on-site. These factors increase the likelihood of ski school being a safe, positive experience for your three- to five-year-old child.

To increase that likelihood, spend time observing the lessons before enrolling your child. The ratio of children to instructors should be 6:1 or less. Are the instructors attentive to the children's needs? Do they progress slowly enough for the children to master each skill? Are they respectful of each child's stamina and ability level? Do they genuinely seem to like the kids?

Some ski resorts will offer all-day ski schools for children three and up, with the programs having an age-appropriate amount of ski instruction, indoor playtime, and nap time. Make sure that your child is comfortable with such an arrangement before enrolling her. And also make sure that her instructors are comfortable with you dropping in to check on your child. Be prepared to take her out of the program if it isn't turning out to be an enjoyable experience for her.

79. Is my child old enough for organized sports and games?

In their zeal to give Mom and Dad a little time off from the kids, many resorts and luxury hotels will offer organized sports and other activities for young children. But because these programs are often unlicensed (resorts are not subject to state licensing requirements, since the parents are assumed to be on-site) and are often staffed by individuals with little or no training in early childhood education, it's often up to you to decide whether or not these activities are appropriate for your children.

The American Academy of Pediatrics recommends supervised but *unstructured* play for children until the age of six. Infant programs do nothing to improve your baby's physical fitness. Nor do children develop motor skills any faster when enrolled in these programs. Long-term results from any organized sports activities for young children have never been demonstrated. Because most children of this age are not coordinated enough to follow directions accurately or to increase skills with practice, enrolling them in organized programs can lead to frustration and a lifelong aversion to the activity they're being asked to partake in.

Look instead for these age-appropriate activities, when evaluating any vacation program for your child that involves organized activities:

1. **A predictable environment.** Good programs recognize each child's level of development, and don't push a child to perform beyond that level.
2. **A noncompetitive environment.** Competition should not be a part of any program, since your children's ability to excel will be based on their developmental readiness.
3. **A safe environment.** Instructors should not be responsible for more than six children between the ages of three and five—preferably fewer. Programs for children under three should include the participation of a parent, and should be about having fun together, not learning new skills.

80. Biking with your kids

If you like to bike, now is the time to travel with your children: From birth to about five years your children will be able to travel safely in a trailer behind you. Beyond that age, the trailer will be too small for your child, but your child will still be too young, for a few years, to tour on her own bike. Bicycles with gears start at twenty inches, too large for your child until she is at least seven or eight, and it's a little unfair to expect a child to enjoy herself on a bike without gears while you breeze along on state-of-the-art equipment.

Trailers are much safer for your child than mounted seats, so much so that mounted seats should never be used. Mounted seats will not protect your child well in the event of a spill. Also, when in a bicycle-mounted seat, your older children may weigh enough to actually cause you to lose your balance if they fall asleep or move around too quickly.

A well-designed trailer for pulling children, on the other hand, will remain upright even if you take a fall. It offers much greater protection to your child, and greater visibility. Trailers come in bright neon colors, and with the addition of a six-foot flag they tend to encourage motorists to give you and your child a wide berth.

When choosing a trailer, look for a design that is easy to hook onto your bicycle, and that folds compactly for travel. Look also for additional features such as sun, wind, and rain protection, to keep your child as comfortable as possible. Minimal safety standards include a five-point harness, a roll bar, and sides that protect children's fingers from the wheels of the trailer. Good designs will provide these safety features in a model that also offers ample windows for your child to look around.

Beyond the safety aspects, your child will have a better view of the passing world in a well-designed trailer, whereas on a mounted seat she has little more to watch than your back. Trailers have room to pack blankets, water bottles, snacks, and toys that can amuse your child in case the scenery gets dull for her. Many trailers will accommodate two children.

When touring with a child under six months, you'll probably need to order an extra-small helmet from your bicycle shop, and plan to use your child's car seat in the trailer until your baby is old enough to hold her head up well.

Even if you are a seasoned cyclist, take time to practice riding with the trailer attached, before your big trip. Curbs and other hazards will need to be negotiated more carefully. You won't be as maneuverable. You will also have a harder time under windy conditions. When you have a choice, try to plan your trip so that you ride upwind first, for an easier time on the way home.

Although more roads are being built with cyclists in mind, you can't count on a wide shoulder, particularly in scenic natural areas. National parks in the Canadian Rockies, for example, offer voluminous shoulders, whereas you'll be risking your life and your child's if you try cycling in Yellowstone, where shoulders are nonexistent and RVs are rampant. Local bicycle shops can be a great resource for your questions about suitable routes and for the latest information on road conditions.

Some children will be fascinated by biking. For others it will feel about as interesting as a long car ride. Like most activities with children, you'll do best if you remain flexible. Choose routes with multiple loop-back options, stop when you need to, and keep your children as involved as possible by singing songs, pointing out sights, and including them in conversations. Start with a two-hour trip before trying extended or overnight touring. It's your children's vacation as much as yours: Try to make sure that they're having as much fun as you are.

Like any outdoor excursion, prepare your children for any kind of weather. Dress them in layers, take rain gear along, and protect them from the sun with sunscreen of SPF 15 or higher, or with long-sleeved clothing if she is younger than six months. A hat with a visor can be worn under your child's helmet to give her face protection.

Your children should always wear helmets. And you should, too, not only to provide a good example, but also to protect your brain so you'll be around to take care of your kids. According to the *New England Journal of Medicine*, helmets reduce the risk of head injuries in a crash by 85 percent. By 1996, thirteen states had passed mandatory bike helmet laws for minors. But don't wait for a law to tell you that helmets are a good idea.

When choosing a helmet, look for American National Standards Institute approval (ANSI), or Snell certification. Your child's helmet should fit level across her brow, and shouldn't shift when buckled. Choose a buckle that is childproof to avoid your child taking it off while riding in the trailer behind you. You can put a hat with a visor underneath your child's helmet to also give her some protection from the sun.

If you have doubts about your children's staying power on your bike tour, go with a tour group that will map out safe routes and provide a support van to pick you up if your child needs a break. Look for an outfitter that has experience with or who offers specific tours for children under five. Ask the group leader about the ages of other children coming along on the tour, to make sure your child has compatible playmates. And be sure to ask about child-related activities that are included in the tour and about any discounts offered to children your child's age.

FOR MORE INFORMATION:

The **National Head Injury Foundation** offers a free booklet on the importance of bicycle helmets, how to buy them, and tips for getting kids to wear them. 333 Turnpike Rd., Southboro, MA 01772.

The **Bicycle Federation of America** has developed a Bicycle Advocate's Action Kit, full of safety tips. To order, call (800) 877-7080.

Backroads has made perhaps the greatest effort of any outfitter to reach families with young children. The company offers a large selection of family-oriented biking tours, complete with backup van and equipment rental, and selects tour leaders with the experience and desire to work with families with very young children. Catalogs of trips are available by writing Backroads, 1516 Fifth St., Berkeley, CA 94710, or by calling (800) GO-ACTIVE.

Chapter 13
Car Camping, Backpacking, and Beyond

If you're new to outdoor adventures, you may feel that it's going to be difficult to learn how to enjoy them, especially now that you're a parent. But with a little practice, they can be a very enjoyable experience for both you and your kids. Camping is also one of the least expensive ways to take a real vacation from your typical daily routine.

If you're an experienced backpacker, on the other hand, you may feel constrained at first by your children. Some outdoor enthusiasts wait to take their kids along until they're able to hike themselves, and to carry their own pack. These parents miss out on some marvelous early experiences, and also miss the opportunity to give their kids a love of the outdoors at an early age. Don't make the same mistake. Although your outdoor experiences will be different, now that you're a parent, they can be just as rewarding in their own way.

81. Car camping made easy

Car camping is pretty much the five-star camping experience for families, since you can bring with you as much stuff as your car can hold. Some families even go whole-hog and rent or buy a recreational vehicle, the equivalent of bringing your house along.

Even with a compact car you'll be able to lug along a roomy tent, gourmet food, a portable crib and high chair, and enough toys to keep your children happy for hours in case it rains.

Unfortunately, the ease of car camping often translates into crowded conditions at more popular destinations. Campsites at popular national parks can give you the feeling that you're camping in the middle of a parking lot. Look for campsites that give your children plenty of protection from traffic, instead of those where you risk your children being run over by an inexperienced RV driver. Develop a preference for state parks and less popular destinations, where crowding will be less of a problem, and try to plan your trips for times other than summer.

Here's a basic list of staples that you don't want to forget to bring:

> **Campsite items:** tent, rain fly, tarp, sleeping pads or mattress, seasonally appropriate sleeping bags or blankets (more below on keeping your children warm through the night), pillows, an old blanket for the kids to sit on outside, folding or camp-style chairs, candle lanterns, flashlights, batteries, first-aid kit, twine, bungee cords, mosquito netting.
> **Kitchen items:** gas stove, frying pan, dutch oven, saucepan, outdoor barbecue tools (long spatula, fork, and tongs), cutting board, all-purpose cooking knife, can opener, bottle opener, matches, portable grill (to barbecue over a wood fire when the flames subside), aluminum foil, strike-anywhere wooden matches, paper towels, plastic bags, garbage bags, seasoning kit that includes oil and favorite spices, eating utensils, plates, cups, ice chest, dishwashing liquid, sponge.
> **Baby items:** diapers, changing pad, baby carrier, seasonally appropriate clothing, toys, spill-proof cup, age-appropriate eating utensils, premoistened wipes, soap and a nail brush (for you, to keep your hands relatively clean when you're feeding or holding your baby). Nice-to-haves: portable crib, and a portable high chair that will hook onto a picnic table, a real luxury at dinnertime.

Kid items: seasonally appropriate clothing, a backpack-style child carrier (for children up to about thirty-five pounds who grow too tired to walk themselves), a child-size pack that your child can fill with her favorite toys, training pants (even kids who've graduated from training pants may need them again), an inflatable or portable potty, and age-appropriate eating utensils.

FOR MORE INFORMATION:

State tourism bureaus are a good place to start for locating good camping areas. They can also refer you to the appropriate state and county park bureaus.

ALABAMA: Department of Tourism, 401 Adams Ave., P.O. Box 4309, Montgomery, AL 36103-4309 (800) 252-2262; (800) 548-2547

ALASKA: Alaska Division of Tourism, P.O. Box 110801, Juneau, AK 99811-0801 (907) 465-2010

ARIZONA: Office of Tourism, 1100 W. Washington, Phoenix, AZ 85007 (800) 842-8257 (602) 542-8687

ARKANSAS: Department of Parks and Tourism, One Capital Mall, Little Rock, AR 72201 (800) 644-4833

CALIFORNIA: Office of Tourism, 801 K St., Sacramento, CA 95814 (800) 862-2543. State park information: (800) 444-7275

COLORADO: Colorado Tourism and Traveling Authority, P.O. Box 3524, Englewood, CO 80155 (800) 265-6723

CONNECTICUT: Development and Tourism, 865 Brook St., Rocky Hill, CT 06067 (800) 282-6863; (203) 258-4355

DELAWARE: Tourism Office, 99 Kings Hwy., P.O. Box 1401, Dover, DE 19903 (800) 441-8846

DISTRICT OF COLUMBIA: Convention and Visitor Center, 1212 New York Ave. NW, Washington, DC 20005 (202) 357-1697, (202) 962-1825, (202) 472-5265

FLORIDA: Division of Tourism, 126 W. Van Buren, Tallahassee, FL 32399-2000 (904) 487-1462

GEORGIA: Department of Industry, Trade and Tourism, P.O. Box 1776, Atlanta, GA 30301 (800) 847-4842, (404) 656-3590

HAWAII: Hawaii Visitor's Bureau, 2270 Kalakaua Ave., Honolulu, HI 96815 (800) 257-2999 (recording), (808) 923-1811
IDAHO: Department of Commerce, P.O. Box 83720, Boise, ID 83720-0093 (800) 635-7820, (208) 334-2470
ILLINOIS: Central Illinois Tourism Council, 629 E. Washington, Springfield, IL 62701 (800) 822-0292, (312) 793-2094
INDIANA: Department of Commerce, Tourism Division, One N. Capital, Ste. 700, Indianapolis, IN 46204 (800) 382-6771, (317) 232-8860
IOWA: Department of Economic Development, Tourism Division, 200 E. Grand Ave., Des Moines, IA 50309 (800) 345-4692, (515) 242-4705
KANSAS: Department of Commerce and Housing, Travel and Tourism Development, 400 SW Hanison, Ste. 1300, Topeka, KS 66603-3712 (800) 252-6727, (913) 296-2009
KENTUCKY: Department of Travel Development, Capitol Plaza Tower, 500 Mero St., Ste. 2200, Frankfort, KY 40601 (800) 225-8747
LOUISIANA: Louisiana Tourism Center, P.O. Box 94291, Baton Rouge, LA 70804-9291 (800) 334-8626; Office of State Parks: (504) 342-8111
MAINE: Publicity Bureau, P.O. Box 2300, Hallowell, ME 04347 (800) 533-9595
MARYLAND: Department of Tourism, 217 E. Red Wood St., 9th Fl., Baltimore, MD 21202 (800) 445-4558
MASSACHUSETTS: Office of Travel and Tourism, 100 Cambridge St., 13th Fl., Boston, MA 02202 (800) 447-6277, (617) 727-3201
MICHIGAN: Michigan Travel Bureau, 333 S. Capitol, Lansing, MI 48909 (800) 543-2937
MINNESOTA: Office of Tourism, 121 E. 7th, Metro Square, St. Paul, MN 55101 (800) 657-3700
MISSISSIPPI: Metro Jackson Convention and Visitor's Bureau, P.O. Box 1450, Jackson, MS 39215-14500 (800) 354-7695, (601) 960-1891
MISSOURI: Division of Tourism, P.O. Box 1055, Jefferson City, MO 65102 (800) 877-1234, (314) 751-4133

MONTANA: Travel Montana, P.O. Box 200533, 1424 9th Ave., Helena, MT 59620 (800) 847-4868

NEBRASKA: Nebraska Tourism, P.O. Box 30370, Lincoln, NE 68509 (402) 471-5497

NEVADA: Commission of Tourism, Capitol Complex, Carson City, NV 89701 (800) 638-2328

NEW HAMPSHIRE: New Hampshire Tourism, P.O. Box 1856, Concord, NH 03302 (603) 271-2665

NEW JERSEY: Office of Travel and Tourism, CN-826, Trenton, NJ 08625 (800) 537-7397

NEW MEXICO: Department of Tourism, Lamy Bldg., 491 Old Santa Fe Trail, Rm. 117, Santa Fe, NM 87503 (505) 827-6465

NEW YORK: Division of Tourism, One Commerce Plaza, Albany, NY 12245 (800) 225-5697, (518) 474-4116

NORTH CAROLINA: Department of Tourism, 430 N. Salisbury St., Raleigh, NC 27611 (800) 847-4862

NORTH DAKOTA: Tourism Division, 604 East Blvd. Ave., Bismarck, ND 58505 (800) 435-5663, (701) 224-2525

OHIO: Department of Tourism and Travel, 77 S. High St., 29th Fl., Columbus, OH 43266 (800) 282-5393, (614) 486-8844

OKLAHOMA: Tourism and Recreation, 241 N. Lincoln, 500 Will Rogers Bldg., Oklahoma City, OK 73105 (405) 521-2406

OREGON: State Office of Tourism, 1115 Commercial St. NE, Salem, OR 97310-1001 (503) 378-6305

PENNSYLVANIA: Travel Department, 453 Forum Building, Harrisburg, PA 17120 (800) 847-4872

PUERTO RICO: Division of Tourism, P.O. Box 4435, Old San Juan Station, San Juan, PR 00905 (809) 721-1712

RHODE ISLAND: Rhode Island Department of Economic Development, 7 Jackson Walkway, Providence, RI 02903 (800) 556-2484, (401) 277-2601

SOUTH CAROLINA: Department of Parks, Recreation and Tourism, 1205 Pendleton St., Columbia, SC 29201 (800) 346-3634, (803) 734-0235

SOUTH DAKOTA: Chamber of Commerce, P.O. Box 747, Rapid City, SD 57709, (800) 487-3223, (605) 343-1744

TENNESSEE: Tennessee Tourist Development, P.O. Box 23170, Nashville, TN 37202-3170 (615) 741-2158

TEXAS: Travel/Information Division, 125 E. 11th St., Austin, TX 78701-2483, (800) 452-9292, (512) 463-8586

UTAH: Travel Council, Council Hall, Capitol Hill, Salt Lake City, UT 84114 (801) 538-1030

VERMONT: Vermont Travel Bureau, 134 State St., Montpelier, VT 05602-3403 (802) 828-3237

VIRGINIA: Virginia Tourism, 901 E. Byrd St., 19th Fl., Richmond, VA 23219 (804) 786-4484 for a travel counselor; (800) 932-5827 to order travel guide and maps. Or contact the state via the World Wide Web at www.virginia.org. The State Parks service operates a separate reservation number and travel counseling; contact them at (800) 933-PARK.

WASHINGTON: Department of Commerce and Economic Development, Tourism and Travel Division, P.O. Box 42500, Olympia, WA 98504-2500 (206) 586-2088

WEST VIRGINIA: Division of Tourism, Parks and Recreation State Capitol Complex, Bldg. 6, Rm. B564, Charleston, WV 25305 (800) 225-5982

WISCONSIN: Wisconsin Travel Information Center, P.O. Box 7606, Madison, WI 53707-7606 (800) 372-2737, (608) 266-2161

WYOMING: Division of Tourism, I-25 at College Drive, Cheyenne, WY 82002 (800) 225-5996

82. About RVs

Depending on your inclination, recreational vehicles (RVs) are either a boon or a bane. They give you the luxury of guaranteed cooking, lavatory, and power facilities, as well as a leakproof roof over your head. But they also remove you from the outdoor experience by forcing you to choose camping areas with RV hookups, and making you dependent on an (often noisy) generator for your needs. Many RV sites offer swimming pools and organized activities, making RV vacations more like staying in a budget hotel than an actual camping experience.

Is an RV right for your family vacation? Here's some questions to ask yourself before you rent or buy:

1. Is someone in your family going to enjoy driving the RV? The experience of driving an RV is something like towing a small house. If you or your spouse aren't comfortable with driving something so large, then you won't enjoy traveling by RV. It's best that you are both comfortable, so you can trade the dual responsibilities of driving and taking care of the children.

2. Is someone in your family going to enjoy managing the ins and outs of the RV's weight requirements, as well as its plumbing, electrical, and propane systems?

   The devil is in the details, and unless you and/or your spouse enjoy the more technical matters involved with RV systems, your trip will be neither safe nor fun. First-time RV families may make the mistake of thinking their home-on-wheels is little more complicated than checking into a hotel, when in reality at least one of you needs to be a self-reliant, Mr. Fix-It type to really enjoy the RV experience.

   The combined weight of water, fuel, passengers, and all of your gear must not exceed recommended levels. That's why it's important to weigh your rig prior to loading to see how much weight you can add; weigh it again after loading to make sure you haven't exceeded safe levels. Proper distribution of that weight is also important for safe driving.

   The wastewater and sewage from sinks, the shower (gray water), and toilet (black water) must drain into separate holding tanks. A monitor panel is usually included with the RV to indicate, the level of water in each tank. It's critical for you to understand and be comfortable with the procedures for both filling and emptying the tanks for you to enjoy a safe RV experience.

   Safe use of appliances requires a thorough understanding of your RV's electrical system, and also requires you to have a passing knowledge of both automobile and home electronics. A separate propane gas system is used in RVs to operate the refrigerator, range, and the furnace. The propane system includes tanks that contain pressurized fuel, plus a system of valves and pipes that supply gas vapor to the major appliances. Obviously you'll need a level of confidence and knowledge in this system to keep it from becoming a hazard to your family.

If these types of details bore both you and your spouse, then RVs are not for you.

3. Do you live in an area where you have many destinations suitable for RV travel within a half-day of your home?

Travel in an RV is not any easier or more interesting to your children than travel by automobile. They still need to be strapped in their safety seats. That means long journeys will be just as challenging. Especially if you're buying your RV, you'll get much more value if you have several destinations close by where you'll be able to enjoy it.

Choose your RV with an eye toward keeping hazards for your small children to a minimum. An RV's efficient use of space for bathroom, kitchen, and sleeping requirements means your child can get into trouble quickly. Plan to bring along a portable gate so that you can keep your children contained in the sleeping area of the RV, an area that's usually relatively easy to childproof, and away from the kitchen area and the chemical toilet.

FOR MORE INFORMATION:

The Directory of RV Rental Dealers (covering the United States, Canada, and Europe) and the brochure "Rental Ventures," which provides tips on touring North America via rental unit, are available for $7.50 postpaid from the Recreational Vehicle Rental Association at (800) 336-0355.

83. Driving tips for RV families

1. **Know your dimensions.** Don't wait until you see the CLEARANCE—8 FEET sign to wonder how high your RV is. Remember to include the height of anything sticking out of the top of your RV, such as an air-conditioning unit.

2. **Practice.** It's hard to spend time in a parking lot with your RV when you're renting by the week, but unless you have prior experience with driving large vehicles, it's a necessity for safe travel. Practice using your mirrors, turning, parking, and backing up until all become second nature to you.

3. **Make wide turns.** Probably the most common mistake you'll make as a novice is forgetting to turn wide. If you do forget, you'll run over curbs and may even cut into a lane of traffic when making a left-hand turn. Practice is the key. When you make each turn, remember to focus on what's happening with the rear of your vehicle. Visualize a path for the rear wheels so that they are both in the lane as you complete your turn.

4. **Learn to use your mirrors.** You need to do without a rearview mirror, and to learn how to interpret what your side mirrors tell you. Know where your blind spots are (have a friend or spouse stand behind and to the sides of your RV until you locate them for yourself). Be extra careful when making lane changes. And always use a spotter to help you back up—your blind spot will be largest immediately behind your vehicle.

5. **Take it slow.** Keep close tabs on how fast you're going down hills (usually the uphill journey in an RV will be slow, anyway). Choose level parking spots without any cars or other obstacles around them until you gain the confidence and experience for negotiating tighter spots.

6. **Keep your children in their safety seats at all times, without exception.** Your RV will feel heavier and safer than a car, and you'll be tempted to take your children out if they complain. Resist that temptation,

and resolve before you leave to always wait until you can pull over safely and stop.

84. Sleeping out

If you don't go the RV route, your tent will be the most important item you bring along. Since portability is not an objective with car camping, go for at least a six-by-eight-foot dome-shape tent: It will hold a queen-size inflatable mattress, with room to spare on the sides for clothing, blankets, and extra kids.

Try renting a tent for a weekend trip before you buy one. You'll discover things about your family's sleeping habits that may surprise you. A tent that seemed large in the store may actually be too small for all of your family's needs. You may find the tent is the perfect place to put your toddler as you set up camp or cook dinner, and decide you need a model with more windows. Or you may decide that a model that includes a small covered area, something like the entrance to an igloo, for taking muddy shoes off and on is worth the extra money when you have kids along. Most retailers of outdoor gear will have a complete line of tents and other equipment for rent.

Some parents recommend that you and your spouse buy sleeping bags that zip together, and that you sleep with your children between you. It's a good way to keep your children warm, but depending on how much they roll around at night, it's definitely not the most restful way to sleep. If you're car camping and don't need to worry about the portability of your sleeping gear, you don't really need to use sleeping bags at all. Down comforters or all-weather quilts can be just as warm, and will give everyone much more freedom to move around in their sleep. Your children can either sleep between you, or on either side of you. If they tend to kick off blankets, zipping them into your down vest or jacket can make for a good makeshift sleeping bag for them.

Unfamiliar sleeping arrangements can have an effect on your child's bathroom habits. It can be intimidating and scary to a child to get out of a warm tent and into the cold night to urinate. Take time to explain to your children what to expect before you go. And be prepared by bringing along training pants even for your potty-trained kids—you'll all sleep better at night.

85. Hikes that work with kids your child's age

From birth to about eighteen months, the distance of your hike is only limited by how far you can walk yourself, since you'll be carrying your child. The carrier you choose will affect how much you and your child enjoy the experience. Here are some things to keep in mind:

1. **Stay with a front-carrier as long as it's comfortable.**

   Choose a carrier that allows your baby to face out and see the world as soon as her neck is strong enough.

   In addition to being your only option until your baby can hold her head up well (about six months or so), front-carriers offer these advantages over backpack-style carriers: They give your baby a better view; they keep you more in touch with her moods and needs; your child is safer from branches and other trail hazards than if you carried her on your back, and the two of you will be able to communicate more easily. Front-carriers also allow you to hike with a lightly-loaded backpack, so that you can help to carry supplies along with carrying your baby.

   After your child reaches fifteen pounds or so, however, carrying all of her weight from your shoulders will be very tiring. Your decision to move to a backpack-style carrier between fifteen and twenty-five pounds will depend on your back, your personal preference, and your ability to find a front-carrier that allows you to distribute at least some of your child's weight to your hips. Look for well-padded shoulder straps and/or a large, functional waistband. Both the Baby Bundler and the Baby Trekker, described on page 59, are good alternatives, or ask children's retailers and outdoor equipment specialists in your area for their suggestions.

2. Go for quality.

Once you shift from a front-carrier to a backpack-style carrier, look for a product that is designed and crafted with the same care as quality outdoor equipment. A good backpack-style carrier will distribute your child's weight as efficiently as the best backpack. A well-fitted carrier will rest your child's weight on your hips, not from your shoulders. Be sure to look for models that provide a sturdy, built-in stand, so you can get the carrier on and off without help from another adult.

A good carrier, with accessories such as additional storage areas and rain shields, can run in excess of $200. It will be worth it if it allows you to backpack and hike with the same ease as you did before you had children. Your best bet is to start with outdoor equipment retailers, who will sell you sturdy products, rather than child supply stores, which will tend to sell products that are fine for around town but are too flimsy for long outdoor trips.

3. Plan for bad weather.

Child carriers aren't ideal in inclement weather, so you'll need to plan ahead for this contingency and choose the best equipment you can to protect your child from the elements.

No front-carrier is equipped with rain protection, so you'll need to provide it yourself. If your baby is still under four months, she will be facing you as you carry her, and your only real option for keeping her dry is to take along a compact umbrella. If she's old enough to hold her head up well and you're carrying her facing out, choose a roomy raincoat with a double zipper for yourself. When it rains, zip her inside the raincoat with you with just her head sticking out. Put a rain hat on her to keep her completely dry and warm. If you plan to carry your child in a backpack-style carrier, choose

a model that has well-designed rain shield for both
vertical and side protection.

4. **Let your child lead.**

From two to four years, your child will likely be walking for part of the trip, and will need to be carried for
part of it. If your child will be walking herself for the
most part, plan to hike no more than two miles a day,
at a rate of about a half-mile per hour. Don't be dis-
couraged or impatient if you need to stop every fifteen
minutes or so for a break of some sort. If your child is
still small enough to be carried, temper your desire to
keep her in the backpack so you can hike at your own
pace, with a deference to her need to walk around and
enjoy herself.

FOR MORE INFORMATION:

Below is a partial list of suppliers for backpack-style carriers
that are built for heavy-duty hiking and backpacking. The most
important qualities to look for will be proper fit, comfort for
your child, adequate safety harnesses, and weather-proofing
capability. Nice-to-haves include extra storage pockets, and the
ability to stand the carrier upright for easy loading.

Before you rent or buy, be sure to try the carrier on with your
child in it. If you're ordering by mail, be sure to get a lenient
return policy that allows you to check the carrier for proper fit.
Antelope Mountain Sports (408) 364-1772 (offers custom-
made carriers)
Kelty K.I.D.S. (800) 423-2320.
L.L. Bean (800) 221-4221
Remond for Babies (800) 426-9244
Tough Traveler (800) GO-TOUGH

86. Backpacking with kids

What about overnight hikes, or longer? When is it safe to bring
your children along? No one will be able to make that decision
for you. Your decision will be based on your experience level,
your first-aid skills, the ages and health of your children, and the

terrain where you plan to backpack. Obviously a trip through a relatively level, temperate area will pose less risk than a trip to areas where a lost child could risk death from exposure.

Before attempting any backpacking trip with your children, make sure that the whole family is comfortable with car camping, and with extended day hikes. If you have a child that will need to be carried (usually a requirement when bringing children under three years of age along) then use these day hikes to test several baby carriers for their comfort over the long haul, for both you and your child.

Remember that a child moving around in a backpack will be more challenging to carry than the same weight in supplies—even if your child is only about twenty-five pounds and you're used to carrying forty, don't plan to carry much else besides the child, except possibly the diaper bag and other miscellaneous baby paraphernalia. That means you'll need at least two adults along for each child that you carry, with one adult responsible for carrying the child, and one for carrying everything else.

87. When you can't carry it all yourself . . .

Let's say the close quarters of car camping—the caravans of RVs with their blazing Coleman lanterns and their loud music and their generators running all night—leave you very unhappy. But you find that you simply can't carry all you'll need to go backpacking, when you need to carry your children, too. What are your options then?

Plenty. Here's a sampler:

1. **Camp after Labor Day weekend.**
   September is still wonderful weather in North America, even as far north as the Yukon; the bugs will be more tolerable; and you'll find that car camping areas will have much more elbow room than they do during the summer months. Take advantage of the fact that your children are still too young to be in school, and go during the school year.

2. Jack-camp.

Jack-camping is a term used for driving and camping wherever you end up. Particularly in the Western states, you can often drive to areas that are nearly as far off the beaten path as any backpacking trip can take you.

The Bureau of Land Management and the National Forest Service maintain many primitive campsites, as do many private forestry companies. These campsites are often accessible only from fire roads or logging roads, which are often not paved, so you'll need to invest in a four-wheel-drive vehicle to be confident about making it in and out. But once you get there, you often can combine the luxuries of car camping with the solitude and beauty of backpacking. You can also just pull off the road and set up camp in many areas. Check at the local Forest Service ranger station or Bureau of Land Management office for details.

You'll need to bring your own drinking water, or to treat the water you find. You and your children will need to make do without cinder-block rest rooms and hot showers. And in some areas, you won't be permitted to build a fire, so bring a stove along. Since you'll have your car, bringing supplies will not be the issue it is with backpacking, and that's a big advantage when camping with children.

3. Go with an outfitter.

Although many tour groups have minimum age requirements on their overnight hiking trips, others don't. You may also be able to persuade a given tour leader to accept your young children if you plan to carry them yourself (small legs can hold up the entire group) and the terrain is not too difficult. Going with an outfitter gives you the luxury of enjoying a walk deep into the wilderness with your children, and knowing that someone else will be hauling all the stuff you need to your campsite.

FOR MORE INFORMATION:

The Sierra Club sponsors over three hundred trips every year. One alternative that's especially good for young families is the Sierra Club's Toddler Tromp, held in Acadia National Park, Maine, each year. Contact the Sierra Club Outing Department at 730 Polk St., San Francisco, CA 94109, or call (415) 977-5630.

The National Wildlife Federation offers week-long programs that include wildlife field trips and nature hikes, many of which are suitable for preschoolers. (800) 245-5484.

4. Hire a llama.

What better way to make sure your child enjoys your wilderness experience than to bring a couple of big animals along with you? A favorite in petting zoos, llamas are extremely good with young children, making them a safer choice than burros or horses at this stage of your child's development. The ecological impact of llamas is minimal, especially when compared with other pack animals. Even very young children can lead them. They're a great way to haul everything you need.

A typical llama packing outfit will offer scheduled tours into wilderness areas (be sure to check the minimum age). They will also drop off and pick up supplies at a designated area for families that want to hike unencumbered. Or they will rent llamas to families who really want to do it all themselves.

FOR MORE INFORMATION:

Contact the International Llama Association at (800) WHY LAMAS to order a free copy of "The Llama Catalog," which includes a list of commercial packers by state. The 800 number is a recording where you can leave your name and address; if you have more specific questions, you can also call the Association at (303) 756-9004.

5. Canoe camp.

Canoe camping allows you to bring the equivalent amount of stuff that you could in a minivan, and to travel as far away from cars and people as you want to with your family along. To be safe, you must first get paddling experience, you must always put everyone in Coast Guard–approved life vests, and you must select a gentle, shallow route. If you take care of those three things, then your canoe trip will be about as safe for your children as taking a bath.

If you're new to canoeing, take a class before you venture out with your family. A well-taught class will give you the good judgment and the safety skills you need to make your family outings successful. For the first several trips, plan to go with an outfitter or with a canoe club. You'll be able to locate these through local retailers of canoe equipment; they should also be able to help you with finding Coast Guard–approved vests for even the smallest members of your family.

FOR MORE INFORMATION:

The American Canoe Association publishes a directory of state and local canoe clubs in the ACA *Canoeing and Kayaking Instruction Manual,* written by Laurie Gullion. Order it at your local outdoor equipment store or contact the ACA at P.O. Box 1190, Newington, VA 22122.

Quetico Discovery Tours offers fully-supported family canoe trips in the Quetico Provincial Park of Ontario, Canada. Guests have ranged in age from eight weeks to eighty-seven years. Each trip is individually tailored for a given family's needs. Quetico Discovery Tours has operated for over twenty years with a perfect safety record. A good alternative for young families who are new to canoeing. Weekly fee: $442 adults; $332 children under 12. (807) 597-2621.

88. Eating "out"

If you're breast-feeding a baby, the only thing you need to worry about when camping or backpacking is to choose layered clothing that allows you to nurse with a minimum of undressing. If your baby is bottle-fed, though, you may want to stick with car camping and day hikes until she is weaned. Premixed formula is heavy to carry, and mixing formula yourself on the trail will be a challenge. Car campers will probably find the convenience of premixed formula and single-use bottles to be worth the extra expense.

Nothing beats a food dehydrator for helping you to bring along nutritious meals for children new to solid food. Simply steam some vegetables before you go, mash them up, and dehydrate them before you leave. Add water when she's ready to eat. It's the best solution for backpacking, when space will be at a premium. Dried cereal flakes and other commercially available dehydrated foods also pack well. Most campgrounds will allow you to bring jars of baby food, even those that ban other kinds of bottles and cans.

If your children have graduated to regular table food, let them participate in the menu planning and food shopping before your trip. If they want to bring items that spoil easily, are heavy to carry, or have the potential of melting in the car and making a big mess, it's a chance for you to explain how camp cooking is different from cooking at home.

Neither chlorine nor iodine treatments for water are recommended for children, and filtering may not rid water of all harmful organisms. Plan to boil your drinking water. Boil the water for at least two minutes at sea level, and eight to ten minutes at elevations above 5,000 feet, to make it safe to drink.

89. Diapers and beyond

If you are car camping, take along the diapers that you normally use for your baby, since space is not an issue. But if you're backpacking, you have a tough decision to make.

Cloth diapers are a reusable resource, and that's good. But they're heavy and messy when wet, and their absorption rate is not very high when compared with disposables. Washing diapers on the trail and hanging them out to dry every night is time-consuming, energy-wasting (you'll need to heat water to get them acceptably clean) and ecologically undesirable (there's the problem of what to do with the waste water when you're done). You'll also be in trouble if it rains, if you're counting on washing and drying diapers along the way.

Of course disposable diapers are even worse news, ecologically speaking. Even the diaper companies know that, and to their credit, they've decreased the amount of material used to manufacture each diaper by nearly 100 percent over the last ten years. They're also working on a compostable diaper, but they're not there yet, so disposables can't be buried in the backcountry. They won't burn, either, except in fires too hot to be politically correct on the trail. (Disposable diaper liners, by the way, have the same sticky issues as disposable diapers: They don't decompose, and they tend to melt rather than burn.)

What's an ethical, ecologically-minded backpacking family to do? First, resolve that if you backpack, you'll be packing dirty diapers out, whether they are disposable or cloth. It's not as bad as it sounds: Some well-traveled hiking trails require backpackers to carry all of their waste back with them, not just their baby's.

But even if you can't really "dispose" of them in the backcountry, disposables offer so many advantages to cloth that it's hard not to recommend them for your camping trip. Disposables have the capacity to hold up to a quart of liquid and still keep your baby dry. You probably won't want to wait that long before changing your baby, but you'll still be able to change her much less often than if she wore cloth diapers. That means you can carry fewer diapers along, and have fewer messy diapers to carry back with you. They are also lighter, both when new and used, and they come with their own waterproof covers, so you don't have to waste space in your pack for separate covers.

The amazing absorption rate of disposables is achieved through chemical processes that you probably don't want to know too much about, and that may irritate your baby's skin. If you normally use cloth, try different brands of disposables for a few days at home to find the least irritating ones before taking them on the trail with you.

Be sure to bring something to act as a changing pad so you don't have to improvise every time you change a diaper. A square of waterproof material that can be wiped off and folded up in a pocket will do nicely. Premoistened wipes are a convenience worth their weight in a pack, and they do burn.

Children who have been potty-trained pose a completely different set of challenges while camping or backpacking. From one camping trip to the next, your child may suddenly get extremely modest and be unable to go outdoors at all. Or she may revert temporarily to an earlier stage and need training pants at night. Pit toilets can be downright scary to a child. And even if you're at a location with flush toilets, they may be crowded, or cold, or have spiders in the corner.

Remain sensitive to your child's feelings, and stay flexible. For insurance against a child who has been so thoroughly potty-trained that she just can't squat and go, take a potty along. Inflate-a-Potty, available through Self Care Catalog at (800) 345-3371, is one alternative you can even bring along in a backpack. And take training pants for every night you plan to sleep out.

90. Bad-weather tips

In Prince Rupert, a town on the Pacific coast of British Columbia, it rains so often that even the tourism brochures are full of smiling people in their raincoats. If you're from the Pacific Northwest, where rain is a fact of life, you go prepared. In other areas, though, a patch of bad weather can catch a family off guard, ruining the trip.

To avoid having that happen to your family, do the following:

1. Dress your children in layers. The first layer is to control moisture on the skin: Choose a light cotton blend for summer; cotton, wool, or synthetic long underwear for winter. The middle layer is to insulate: Choose

long-sleeved shirts and pants for your children that hold in the warmth. The outer layer is to protect from the elements, and should be both waterproof and wind-proof. Always pack extra socks for your child, and an extra insulating layer in case the first one gets wet.

2. Buy the best rain gear for you and your children that you can afford, if you are planning to hike in any area where rain is possible. One-piece rain suits for children offer the least likelihood of leaks and provide good all-body protection from the wind, too.

3. Choose a tent that offers plenty of room if children need to be inside it for an afternoon shower, and pack a tarp to give your family some extra protected space outside of the tent, and where you'll also be able to use a stove. Let your children pack their own toys, to be taken out only if it rains. Always pack a rain fly for your tent.

4. For children who are walking, waterproof their boots before the trip. Sew gloves and hats onto your children's sleeves to avoid them getting lost or dropping in a puddle.

5. Remember that children who are being carried on a hike will be doing far less exercise than you, and will feel the drop in temperature that accompanies rain more keenly than you do. Dress them in an extra layer or two, and check frequently to be sure that the carrier's rain shield is protecting them adequately from getting wet.

6. Take your children's complaints about being cold seriously. Children are far more susceptible to hypothermia than adults; even with the best of equipment and rain gear it will be difficult to keep them completely warm and dry in a heavy downpour.

7. If you plan a winter hike over snow, prepare against potential sunburn and snowblindness. Wait to take these trips until your baby is old enough to wear sun-

screen (six months or older) and will tolerate wearing sunglasses. Choose glasses that offer UV protection.

8. Do consider postponing any trip when there is a forecast of heavy, steady rain, and avoid high-altitude trips that risk your family being exposed to unexpected snowstorms.

FOR MORE INFORMATION:

Frostline Kits markets sewing kits for outdoor clothing, and has products to keep your children warm and dry from age six months. If you like to sew, it's a good way to economize as your children go through their rapid-growth period. (800) KITS USA.

91. The truth about bug juice

Few things will be more disturbing on your outdoor adventure than the sight of mosquitoes dive-bombing your children's tender skin. But before you reach for the insect repellent to ward them off, make sure you're armed with the facts.

United States–manufactured products that are classified as "insect repellents" by the Environmental Protection Agency usually include diethyltoluamide, commonly known as DEET. Over half of the DEET applied to your children's skin will be absorbed rapidly and enter the bloodstream. While it's easily absorbed, it isn't easy to get rid of. Some portion of the chemical will be stored in your children's bodies for months. It may never be completely eliminated, and frequent use will cause a buildup of its toxic effects. DEET has been implicated in a number of severe poisonings (about five thousand a year) and has caused brain damage in young children. Over three-fourths of reported poisonings are in children under six. In some cases, DEET may cause a range of other troubling effects, including irritability, lethargy, dizziness, headaches, nausea, brain swelling, cardiorespiratory arrest, scarring skin rashes, muscle cramps, and convulsions.

Some parents knowingly risk the hazards of DEET in the mistaken belief that their children will then be protected from Lyme disease. They won't be. Even 100 percent DEET products, far too toxic for any child, will repel ticks only about 75 percent of the time, so you'll still need to check your child's body for ticks whether you use repellent or not. Also be aware that Lyme disease is completely preventable by examining your children's skin every twelve hours and gently removing with tweezers any ticks that you find. It takes roughly twenty-four hours for the disease-causing bacterium to make its way out of the tick's body and into your child's.

What about mosquitoes, black flies, and those other pesky insects commonly known as "no-see-ums"? While these insects aren't disease-causing in North America, they can certainly ruin your outdoor experience. Fortunately, there are plenty of strategies for making sure they don't, that also don't require you to risk exposing your children to potentially harmful substances.

Below is a range of bug-repelling tactics, in order of their potential danger and toxicity to your child, ranging from insect diplomacy to all-out nuclear war:

1. **Good timing.** Mosquito appetites are at their peak at dusk and at dawn. Time your activities so that your children can play quietly in the tent or underneath mosquito netting until the bugs lose their bite.

2. **The right clothing.** Dress your children (and yourself) in long-sleeved clothing. If you're wearing just one layer, choose clothing made from tightly-woven cotton fabric that mosquitoes can't bite through. Denim is a good choice. Tuck pants into socks to avoid bites around the ankles. Some parents have also found that sewing strings of yarn to the brim of their children's hats discourages bugs from attacking the face. If you're traveling to very buggy areas, bring mosquito netting, too. Tightly woven clothing barriers can be 100% effective against mosquitoes, midges, and black flies, and just as effective as DEET against ticks.

3. **The Maine method.** In the North Woods, a marshy area of Maine that stretches north from Augusta, swarms of black flies will descend on anyone who

walks outside from May to November. If it's too hot to cover up, then take a tip from old Maine saws and cover your children's exposed areas with baby oil. Mainers just slap it on and go about their business. The bugs drown before they bite. One hundred percent effective against black flies; less so against mosquitoes. One hundred percent safe.

4. **Avon calling.** Avon Skin-so-Soft bath oil has long been suspected of having repellent properties. Probably it works in much the same way as the Maine method, by drowning the critters; insects may also dislike its scent. Its effectiveness is high when applied thickly enough to act as a physical barrier. It's also safe to use, although you should not confuse this product with the one Avon markets as an actual insect repellent. The insect repellent version of Skin-so-Soft contains inert ingredients with unknown side effects.

5. **Go natural.** Citronella is a widely used repellent oil. Its pungent extract is especially powerful against mosquitoes and flies. Eucalyptus and lemongrass have sharp odors that insects dislike.

   Although products that contain these ingredients are undoubtedly safer than DEET, they're not necessarily risk-free. Natural formulations can make no claims of either safety or effectiveness, because technically they're not classified as repellents. Your child may also have an allergic reaction to these products, so be sure to test a small patch of skin before slathering them on. But generally they'll offer fair protection, and they have caused few complaints from parents. Avoid products that contain pennyroyal—the main ingredient in dog flea collars—or catnip. Both can be toxic to children.

6. **(Somewhat risky) DEET on clothing only.** Cotton bands soaked in DEET solution and left to dry will retain repellent properties, and can be tied around

wrists and ankles to ward off bugs. You'll be exposing your children to potentially harmful fumes, and you should avoid applying DEET to clothing that will be in direct contact with your children's skin. You should also avoid without exception putting DEET-soaked clothing anywhere near where your child might get it into her mouth. If you decide to use this method, then be sure to choose a very low-percentage DEET product, 10 percent or less, which will probably be nearly as effective as higher concentrations, since it remains on the cloth instead of being absorbed by the skin.

7. **(Not recommended) DEET on the skin.** DEET repellents come in a range of concentrations, from 7 percent to 100 percent by volume. The American Academy of Pediatrics recommends that children never be exposed to any product with more than 10 percent DEET. Usually products with under 10 percent DEET will be designated as being made for children.

   There is really no compelling reason to apply DEET directly to your children's skin. Even if you plan to canoe through the Florida Everglades in peak mosquito season, and have decided that nonchemical methods just aren't enough, DEET-permeated bands of cloth can be just as effective, and are potentially less harmful than DEET applied directly to the skin.

8. **(Dangerous in all cases) High-concentration DEET.** Don't under any circumstances expose your child to DEET products in concentrations over 10 percent. There is simply no need to gamble your child's health when there are equally effective remedies that carry far less risk.

92. Lessons that will serve your kids forever

Here are three lifelong lessons you give your children while camping and backpacking with them—all things that they can begin to learn at a very early age:

1. **Respect for nature.** Talk to your kids, in camp and on the trail. Even before they are old enough to talk back, children will be curious about what they see. Even things that seem silly, like pointing to a tree and saying, "That's a tree!" can keep a baby incredibly involved when you're hiking.

   As your children get older, you can point out the different varieties of fauna, or show them spoor and other signs of animals that have passed the same way. Take time to explain what you see as you walk along, in terms your children can understand. An eroded hillside, a burnt-out tree trunk, or a seed pod hitching a ride on your child's hat all have their stories to tell.

   For rest stops, a good learning game that keeps your kids still and quiet is to take a piece of string or rope from your pack and make a circle on the ground with it, a couple of feet in diameter. Invite your children to look inside the circle and to count the things they find. At first they will need your help, but gradually they'll begin to see the incredible variety of things that a two-foot circle can contain, particularly on forested trails: decaying leaves; pieces of wood; ants, worms, pillbugs, and beetles, and more. At night, invite your children to listen and identify the sounds that surround your campsite. After a few trips, unfamiliar sounds will grow familiar, and even comforting.

   Although singing, playing games, and other means of distracting children from temporary bouts of boredom all have their uses on the trail, the best way to keep your children happy is to show them why you've actually come on this trip in the first place. Involving your children in what's happening around them is the best strategy of all for successful outdoor experiences, and will instill in your children a love of nature that will last a lifetime.

2. **Respect for others.** Teach your children to leave the wilderness better than they found it, by packing out

not only your own things but also other people's litter. Expect your children to help as soon as they are old enough to carry their own small pack.

Avoid bright lights and large fires; opt for low-impact candle lanterns and fires just large enough to meet your needs instead. Explain to your children why you are doing so.

As soon as your children are old enough to walk on the trails themselves, teach them to stay on the trail and to never cut through a switchback, and explain to them how going off of the trail can cause erosion and ruin the area for both people and animals.

By taking time to show your children by your own example about low-impact camping, you'll also be teaching them respect for the people who'll be coming to the area after you leave.

3. **Self-reliance.** Camping and backpacking are all about learning how to take care of yourself, and that's a wonderful lesson to teach your children.

Start to give your children chores to do when they're eighteen months to two years old, and try to increase that level of responsibility every time you camp. Talk to your children before you leave, and ask them how they'd like to help. In areas that allow you to gather your own wood for fires, a good first responsibility for your child is to help find tinder and kindling. Children also like to carry their own pack as soon as they are able. Give them something important to carry, like a small first-aid kit, a flashlight, or a map of the trail. You'll not only be teaching self-reliance, but also giving your children a reason to stay involved with your trip so they enjoy themselves.

93. Survival skills for your child to memorize

Teach your children these rules as soon as they are old enough to be hiking and playing by themselves when you camp:

1. **Hug a tree.** If you get lost, stay in one place and wait for help.
2. **Take a garbage bag and a whistle with you whenever you leave camp.** If you do get lost, make a hole in the side of the bag for your face, cover the rest of your body with the bag, and keep the top of your head covered to stay warm at night. Blow on the whistle, which will require a lot less energy than yelling for help.
3. **Make yourself big.** Wear bright clothes. Find a clearing and make an SOS sign using sticks and rocks.
4. **Leave a footprint behind.** Before you go camping, remind your parents to make a footprint in a piece of aluminum foil of the shoes you'll be wearing, and take it along. It will help rescuers track you down.

The rules were developed by tracker Ab Taylor and writer Tom Jacobs in 1981, after a nine-year-old boy died of exposure only two miles from his campground. They've saved the lives of many children since. They are printed here with permission from the Hug-a-Tree-and-Survive foundation.

Chapter 14
International Travel

Ever wonder why your vacations as a kid went so smoothly? Ask your mom.

—My Mom

There's no reason to cross international travel off your list until your kids are older, especially if you have relatives in other countries who are eager to meet your children. You'll just need to be a little more self-sufficient than usual, and to plan a little more carefully to make sure you have the supplies you need and that you all stay healthy.

You may get a lot of unnecessary advice from well-meaning acquaintances, people who wouldn't dream of taking their own children on such a long trip. Don't let anyone worry you about your plans—only you can decide what's an appropriate destination for your family. People have been raising happy, healthy babies all over the world for a long time, and you'll be giving your family experiences to last a lifetime.

94. Five secrets for stress-free international vacations

One way to let go of travel stress is to give your problems to someone else. Let a tour operator, such as those listed on page 46, handle the myriad details. The risk, of course, is that you and your children will be insulated from the culture you've come to visit. You run the danger of being so well taken care of that you might as well have stayed at home.

Let's assume that organized tours, group travel, and/or all-inclusive packages are not for you. You want to experience the country you're visiting firsthand, and to give your family the opportunity to do the same. Is it still possible to have a good time with small children along? Of course it is.

If you have fond memories of your vagabond existence during your junior year abroad, though, when you thought nothing of sleeping in the seat of a third-class train for days to get from Istanbul to Madrid, then you need to make peace with the fact that a trip with your children along is going to feel a little different.

But not *too* different. With just a few changes, you'll be able to travel abroad with your children in nearly the same style that you would on your own. Here are some ways to keep a feeling of spontaneity and wonder, even if you will need a little up-front planning:

1. **Take the easy way out.** On every international trip you and your family will be faced with choices of how to get to where you're going, where to stay, where to eat, and what to do next. In all cases, ask yourself "What feels easiest?" Then do it. Making things as easy as possible must be your first priority when traveling with small children. Not "What's the best deal?" Not "Do I have to see this particular (cathedral, temple, museum) now or never see it again in my life?" Free your mind of all other priorities and take the easy way out. You'll end up spending more money for taxis instead of waiting for a bus, or renting a car instead of figuring out a train schedule. And you'll end up having a lot more fun, too.

2. **Think in stars instead of circles.** Most of us tend to put together travel itineraries that would be in the shape of a big circle if you drew them on a map. With

children, you'll want to plan trips that resemble a star instead. Establish a home base in the middle, and make short trips back and forth to points of interest in the area. You'll have a place to call home that your children will grow accustomed to. You'll be able to leave part of your luggage behind and travel light. You'll get to know the neighborhood, so you'll know where to stock up on supplies like diapers and baby oil. And you'll be able to establish a relationship with your hotelier, who can help with baby-sitting references, family-friendly restaurants, and with other questions you may have.

3. **Call ahead.** When you decide to stay overnight on one of your trips away from your home base, your options may be limited, so it's best to make reservations at least a day in advance. For example, many of those charming bed-and-breakfasts in the British Isles don't allow children, period.

4. **Split up.** If you're traveling with your spouse or another adult, plan separate activities for an afternoon or two each week. One of you can have an uninterrupted visit to the Prado, the Louvre, or the Tokyo National Museum—all places that children will probably not be happy for more than an hour or so. The other parent will have a special time to be alone with the children, which can be a great experience in its own right. You'll both be refreshed.

5. **Slow down.** Don't plan every minute of every day. In fact, don't plan activities that take more than half a day. Spend the other half in a public area—a plaza or park or courtyard. Give your children space to play, give yourselves a rest, and wait. Something good will happen. Even if you've been to a country many, many times before, your children will transform your experience. People will speak with you who normally would be put off by shyness or by a language barrier. By making time for these unplanned encounters, you'll also make time for some of the richest experiences of your trip.

95. What to bring, what to leave home

Even a few years ago, you may have had trouble finding baby and child supplies overseas that you took for granted in the United States. No more. Worldwide distribution channels are making products like disposable diapers, formula, and other baby products easily available in all but the most far-flung destinations. Here's the lowdown on some commonly needed items:

Formula. You can contact the customer information number of the manufacturer of your baby's formula for help on whether the formula will be available in the country you're visiting. Each major formula manufacturer will handle your request a little bit differently.

Customer representatives of Mead-Johnson, makers of Enfamil products, at (800) 222-9123, will ask you which countries you'll be visiting, and which formula your baby uses. They will then advise you whether or not the product is available in these countries. If your baby's brand of formula is not shipped to the country you're visiting, Enfamil representatives will not suggest alternative products, but will refer you instead to your pediatrician.

If your baby uses Similac, call Ross Products at (800) 227-5767, where customer representatives will either connect you with their international division at Ross's parent company, Abbot Laboratories, for more information, or take your request for information and call you back. Company representatives claim that they will give you not only the countries, but even the cities within a given country where you will be able to buy Similac formula.

Carnation does not ship its infant formula brands internationally, but its parent company since 1985 has been Nestlé, the Swiss food conglomerate that has been criticized in the past for its heavy-handed tactics in marketing formula in underdeveloped countries. Nestlé's marketing clout has been bad news for a lot of mothers and children without access to clean water, but it does mean that you'll find formula in countries where you'd normally think it wouldn't be available. Nestlé holds the largest share of the formula market outside of the United

States. Carnation customer representatives at (800) 782-7766 will help you to identify Nestlé formulas that most closely match the Carnation formula your baby uses, that are additionally available in the countries you plan to visit.

It's a good idea to check with your pediatrician on what other products closely correspond with your baby's current formula, so that you have the broadest range of choices while traveling. Although each formula varies slightly in taste and chemical composition, you should be able to use many formulas interchangeably. Many pediatricians do recommend that you try to stay with iron-fortified formulas, though, since formulas based on cow's milk will be deficient without added iron.

You will need to make sure that the water you use to make the formula is safe, when you're traveling to a country where premixed formula is not available and tap water is risky to drink. Bottled water is safest, followed by water that has been boiled vigorously. Bring or purchase an immersion coil or heating element for in-room boiling—be sure also to bring an electric adapter for use in the countries you visit. Filtering combined with chlorine and iodine treatments are less effective than boiling, and also introduce undesirable chemicals into your baby. Use these purification methods only as a last resort, and be sure to read all warnings and to follow the manufacturer's instructions carefully.

Child safety seats. International automobile rental agencies will provide you with information on where child safety seats in automobiles are mandatory, if you tell them which countries you plan to drive in, and will usually rent seats wherever they rent cars. It's still best to bring your own so that you can use it on the plane, however.

You are very unlikely to encounter any situation where your United States–approved child safety seat doesn't meet local safety standards. Canada is the only possible exception.

In Canada, parents are required to secure safety seats with an additional tether strap that is bolted to the car. The tether strap does away with problems associated with different seat belt designs in automobiles, since the child's seat is firmly anchored to the car by its own, specially-designed strap. The tether also allows the same design of safety seat to pass more rigorous crash tests than seats anchored only with safety belts.

You will probably not be cited as a U.S. tourist driving in Canada if you don't comply with the tether strap provision. The law provides for many exceptions for non-Canadian, short-term travelers. For complete information on the requirements in your particular case, contact Transport Canada at (613) 998-2352.

Some U.S. manufacturers, among them Gerry Baby Products, sell tether straps to retrofit your U.S.-built car seat. You can order them by calling (800) 362-3200. You will need to check with your seat manufacturer whether your particular model of seat has the hole for the tether, and you'll need to have the actual installation completed by an automobile dealership or repair store.

Even when not traveling in Canada, you may want to investigate installing a safety strap, especially if you drive a make of car with scoop-shape bucket seats, and have had trouble installing your car seat securely using conventional seat belts.

Cribs. If you plan to stay in any accommodation other than a large, Western-style chain hotel, you won't be able to count on getting a crib in your room. If your children are at an age where they are likely to fall out of a regular bed or a cot, invest in a portable railing and take it along with you. You can find railings in child supply stores that are light and that fold up easily for less than $30.

If you plan to rent a car, bring along a portable crib that can double as a playpen. It will be well worth the extra space in your car to give you a little peace of mind, and to give your child a familiar place to sleep.

High chairs. High chairs or booster seats in restaurants are few and far between outside of North America. Plan to take along an alternative—a place where your child can sit, eat, and even sleep comfortably while you're out. Your choices include these:

1. A simple restraining strap. It's easy to carry and often useful to strap your child into an available chair as soon as she is strong enough to sit up herself.

2. A portable high chair. If you bring one that is designed to be hooked onto a table, be sure that the table is sturdy enough to handle the weight of your child. Another alternative is the Comfort Seat, available from The Right Start at (800) 548-8531, which consists of a cloth "seat" plus a wide belt that you can use to fasten your child securely into a restaurant chair.
3. A stroller. It's not the best place for eating, especially if your child insists on feeding herself, but it's workable. Not all restaurants will allow you to bring a stroller inside, however.

Child carriers. If a sling, front-carrier, or backpack are comfortable ways for you and your baby to get around, by all means bring it along with you. In countries where wheelchair access laws haven't been enacted (that is, most of the world) you'll be lugging your stroller up and down stairs a great deal, especially when using the otherwise excellent public transit systems in Japan and most of Europe. You'll want an alternative to your stroller in these cases, and also for any scheduled or unscheduled walks off of smoothly paved roads.

Strollers. If your child will sleep in one, strollers are extremely handy. It will be helpful to get you and your children around in airports. Check it at the gate, to be delivered at the gate at your destination, if airport security allows it. For more than one child of stroller age, tandem strollers will fold up better than side-by-side models.

Although umbrella strollers are by far the lightest and most compact, they are not too efficient on rough roads or on cobblestone streets, they aren't very comfortable to sleep in, and they don't offer much protection from the elements. If you can afford the space (that is, you're staying in one place or driving from destination to destination) bring along a sturdier model.

Potties. If you travel in a country where toilet facilities are usually flush with the floor and where you squat on footrests that are an adult's shoulder-width apart (in other words, in most of Asia, as well as some countries in Africa and Europe), then going to the bathroom can be intimidating for your child. Take a potty chair along that has been designed for travel. If your child is too old for a potty chair, look for a Western-style toilet at the end of the row of stalls in public rest rooms: In large cities, at least, you'll usually find one.

It's also good to always be prepared with a package of paper tissues to be used as toilet paper, and a handkerchief for drying hands after washing them. Many countries, particularly in Asia, don't supply these at public facilities.

Diapers. If you're worried about finding diapers where you're going, take a suitcase of disposables and use the empty case to carry your purchases on the way back. If you don't want to bother with the luggage, though, remember that wherever you go, you can be certain that people have babies, and have devised a method for keeping them comfortable until they're toilet trained.

You're also likely to have the same major disposable brands to choose from that are available in the United States, plus some local alternatives. To find the right size diaper for your baby in countries using metric weights, multiply your baby's weight by .45 to convert to kilograms.

Disposables are now about 90 percent of the U.S. diaper market, and so much more convenient for travel that you may not look for alternatives beyond them. If you plan to stay in one location in your international trip, though, and prefer cloth, then bring about one week's supply and try to investigate laundry facilities before you leave. Your hotel may be able to locate a local diaper service for you, or may offer to wash diapers in-house along with its other cleaning services.

Below is a list, provided by U.S. manufacturers of disposable diapers, of the countries where they sold their products in 1996. Some of the countries listed aren't even recognized by the United Nations, yet still manage to be recognized by the makers of Pampers and Huggies. A spokesperson at one company said that the products they sell are virtually identical to the U.S.-made goods, except for about a six-month time lag in the introduction of a new product.

You'll also usually have plenty of local brands to choose from. To avoid a problem with tabs that don't really stay closed, bring along a few Velcro-fastened diaper wraps for your baby to wear over the disposables you buy.

American Samoa	Guam	Paraguay
Anguilla	Guatemala	Peru
Antigua	Guyana	Philippines
Argentina	Haiti	Puerto Rico
Aruba	Holland	Qatar
Australia	Honduras	Romania
Azores	Hong Kong	Russia
Bahamas	India	St. Kitts
Bahrain	Ireland	St. Maarten
Barbados	Israel	St. Pierre
Belgium	Italy	St. Vincent
Belize	Jamaica	Saudi Arabia
Bermuda	Japan	Senegal
Bolivia	Korea	Singapore
Bonaire	Kuwait	Slovenia
Bophuthatswana	Latvia	Solomon Islands
Botswana	Lebanon	South Africa
Brazil	Lesotho	Sri Lanka
Bulgaria	Lithuania	Suriname
Canada	Luxembourg	Swaziland
Cayman Islands	Macao	Switzerland
Chile	Malawi	Taiwan
Ciskei	Malaysia	Thailand
Colombia	Mariana Islands	Togo
Costa Rica	Martinique	Transkei
Croatia	Mauritius	Trinidad and Tobago
Curaçao	Mexico	Turks Island
Cyprus	Montserrat	United Arab Emirates
Dominica	Namibia	United Kingdom
Dominican Republic	Nauru Islands	United States
Ecuador	Nicaragua	Uruguay
Egypt	New Britain	Vanuatu
El Salvador	New Caledonia	Venda
Fiji Islands	New Zealand	Venezuela
France	Oman	Virgin Islands
French Polynesia	Pakistan	Yemen
Germany	Palau Islands	Zimbabwe
Greece	Panama	
Grenada	Papua New Guinea	

96. Public transit vs. renting a car

International train travel has more or less the same good and bad elements as domestic train travel, only you also want to factor in how easy or difficult your alternative modes of transportation are. For much of Central and South America, most of Africa, and all of Europe (with the possible exception of Italy, where roads are narrow and drivers aggressive) renting a car will nearly always be an easier way to get around with children. Even if you travel light, you'll be carrying children along with your luggage. Strollers and portable cribs can be such a convenience that you may want to bring them along, too. With this amount of stuff, even the most intrepid minimalist will find travel by car incomparably easier, when you travel to a country where the roads are good and relatively uncongested.

There are several notable exceptions to the rent-a-car rule. You can plan to stay in one place for your visit, and take a taxi or limousine to get there from the airport. If you're two adults traveling with one child, you'll probably be able to manage on a train or bus, especially if your child is self-propelling.

And almost anywhere in Asia, public transportation will be more convenient than driving. In Japan, for example, which arguably has the best road system in East Asia, any road that isn't a superhighway is extremely narrow, usually gridlocked, and nameless (the Japanese name their blocks, instead of the streets that run between them). In several Southeast Asian countries, notably Indonesia, Thailand, Malaysia, and the Philippines, traffic congestion can be so bad in the major cities that a two-mile ride can take two hours. Travel as lightly as you can and take public transportation. Try to avoid rail passes: They aren't economical unless you plan to travel more than you probably should with small children. Stick with a simple itinerary and single-destination tickets.

97. Breast-feeding abroad

If you are breast-feeding your baby, you're not only giving her the best nutrition in the world, you're also carrying with you a food source that is perfect for traveling: always available, abundant, sterile, and just the right temperature. Your baby will also have fewer bowel movements than a formula-fed baby, always a big perk on a crowded plane. And you will be providing her with a constant and familiar source of comfort, and a sense of home, wherever and however far you travel.

Your baby's nutritional requirements are met by breast milk alone for the first year of your child's life, so if during this time you are considering traveling to areas where clean food and safe water aren't always available, you can delay the introduction of solid food, or reintroduce nursing sessions that you have begun to replace with meals, with no adverse nutritional effects. Just be sure to take care of yourself. Remember to eat well. Drink only bottled or boiled water, and never eat uncooked foods. An illness that requires you to take antibiotics or other drugs may affect your ability to nurse safely.

If you're traveling to a hot country and want to supplement your baby's breast milk diet with water, use bottled water when it's available. Your next best choice is boiled water. Don't give your baby water that's been treated either with chlorine or iodine, unless it's your only choice. Also, remember that your baby has a strong swallowing reflex—when washing her hair or bathing her, pay extra attention to keep the water from her face and mouth, to avoid having her swallow contaminated water.

In general, your experiences with breast-feeding your baby in public while traveling in another country will be positive ones. Unlike the United States, where breast-feeding is sometimes seen as an unnatural act, most of the rest of the world sees it as completely normal. Your most common reaction will be no reaction at all. There will be exceptions, however, and these will always surprise you.

In Europe, you'll encounter the most vocal reactions in Great Britain, where people may feel comfortable about expressing their opinions—not always favorable—about seeing you nursing in a public area. In France, Spain, and Italy you're unlikely to encounter any reaction at all. In Scandinavia, Germany, and the Benelux areas of the Continent, breast-feeding is considered a private experience, but in these countries you will also be able to take advantage of areas set aside for just that purpose. In German department stores, ask for the *Entwicklungsraum*, which usually offers a clean and spacious place to nurse.

In some developing countries, breast-feeding is associated with being a member of a lower economic class, and so you may attract attention and curiosity simply by confounding expectations, as an American tourist who also breast-feeds. Oddly enough, in the very countries where Western women usually find it most difficult to travel, such as those with strict Muslim codes of dress and behavior for women, you will often have the most positive experiences as a nursing mother. Other women may express their approval and stop to admire your baby—your relationship with your nursing child can even act as a bridge to a culture that would otherwise be all but inaccessible to you.

As a nursing mother who is also an international traveler, you probably already have a sense of adventure, as well as a good dose of self-confidence about your parenting skills. Use them both to your advantage, if and when you have an unexpected reaction to your breast-feeding from the people around you. Remember that part of the reason why we travel is to have just these kinds of cross-cultural experiences. Try to learn from them instead of simply reacting to them.

FOR MORE INFORMATION:

Contact **La Leche League International** at (800) LA-LECHE for help with any additional questions you have about breast-feeding while traveling.

For immediate, up-to-date, anecdotal help from other parents on what you can expect in a given country, try posting your question to the appropriate travel discussion groups on CompuServe, America Online, or Usenet newsgroups misc.kids or the rec.travel hierarchy.

98. What immunizations does my child need?

The moment you take your child outside the front door, you're exposing her to new things, some of them potentially harmful.

Does that mean you never open the front door? Of course not. You need to find the right balance of caution and confidence, of risk and reward, for your particular family. Part of that balance will be how to protect your child from harmful and potentially life-threatening diseases while traveling.

Many doctors will urge that you delay all international travel until your baby has completed her complete round of immunizations—a recommendation that will keep you from traveling until all of your children are four years old. Other doctors will advise that you need not unduly delay your travel plans, since some diseases that are regularly immunized against are not life-threatening, particularly in children. Some immunized diseases, like polio, have now been declared eradicated in much of the world, including all of North and South America, making it highly unlikely that your baby will contract this disease even if she travels before being immunized against it. And since much of the world has health standards that equal or even surpass those of the United States, a blanket recommendation to delay all international travel is more than a little paranoiac.

With something as important as your child's health at risk, though, it's important that you are well-informed. In the end it will be you who will need to decide whether travel to a particular area is advisable, and you and your child who will need to be prepared for the consequences of your decision.

Here are some commonsense guidelines when planning trips to tropical or developing countries:

1. Call the Centers for Disease Control's International Traveler's Hotline, at (404) 332-4555, to learn what immunizations you'll need and what medical precautions you should take in the countries you plan to visit.
2. Ask your pediatrician for advice, but don't stop there. Also consult with a clinic that specializes in international travel to obtain the best information on what is required to protect your child in a given country. Either your doctor or your travel agent should be able to refer you to a specialized clinic near you.

3. Tetanus is a leading cause of death in many developing countries, and is particularly prevalent in infants. Although tetanus is often associated with deep wounds, even superficial scratches can be infected. If you plan to travel before your baby receives her complete round of immunizations, ask your doctor or a specialist about the risks associated with such travel.

   In any case, do not ever allow your child to walk barefoot or to crawl on the ground without protecting her skin from possible abrasions, particularly when traveling to tropical countries or agricultural areas where animal manure is used for fertilizer.

4. If you plan to travel to countries where yellow fever immunization is mandatory, ask your pediatrician when this vaccine can be safely given—usually not before nine months. The immunization is highly effective and lasts ten years. Allow at least ten days before you travel, for the immunization to take effect and for your children to get over any adverse reactions.

5. Many diseases that are prevalent in developing countries have no immunizations available, so you'll need to use other methods for protecting your children from contracting them. Have a clear understanding of the risks before you finalize your travel plans, and be scrupulous about clean water and safe food when you are there.

99. Special health and safety concerns

Be alert for these potential health and safety hazards with your children when taking them on an international trip.

Unlike domestic flights, many international flights allow smoking, and it's especially hard to find nonsmoking flights for Asia-bound destinations. Make sure to ask, and to book nonsmoking flights whenever they are available to avoid exposing your children to secondhand smoke.

Nonsmoking restaurants and even nonsmoking sections of restaurants are few and far between in other countries. Now that secondhand smoke has been indisputably linked to increased risk of bronchitis, asthma, and Sudden Infant Death Syndrome, you need to take active measures to guard your children from smoking's ill effects. Dine at off-peak hours and in well-ventilated restaurants whenever possible.

If your child is walking, take along a safety harness and walking tether, even if you usually don't use one. Once you leave our litigious land, you can't count on always finding safety features like guard railings on stairs or barriers on balconies, and you may welcome having a handy way to keep your child safe. You'll also be better off in a crowd: It will also be particularly hard on your child if she is inadvertently separated from you in a country where she can't speak the language. Tethers may look strange or be unappealing to you, but they make good sense in places where you're otherwise putting your child at risk. Most models can also double as safety straps when you seat your child in a restaurant.

Be careful to check your hotel's safety precautions, since safety features you've learned to take for granted here may not be available everywhere. Is there a sprinkler system and/or a smoke detector in your room? Is there a safe and accessible fire escape route that you can manage while carrying your children who are too small to walk themselves to safety? Do the doors and windows lock, and are the locks out of the reach of your children's curious fingers? If the answer to any of these questions is "no," then choose another hotel.

If you plan to drive, get an international driver's license before you go. Obtain a copy of local driving laws, and learn them before you ever start the car. Rights-of-way laws are particularly important to understand, as these vary by country, and misunderstanding them can easily lead to accidents.

If you visit a country where you'll be driving on the left side of the road, don't rent your car from the airport. You'll be tired, and airports are difficult and congested places to learn new driving skills. Wait until you get to your hotel, and ask that the car be delivered to you there, preferably at a time when there is very little traffic so you'll be able to practice. Remember that even walking across a street requires you and your children to look in unfamiliar places for hazards, so stay alert.

Of course you should plan to use your children's automobile safety seats on the airplane, and to install them in the car you rent even if they are not mandatory in the countries you visit. But in some particularly challenging destinations, you may find that the rental cars from local companies will come without seat belts, making your children's safety seats useless. To avoid that problem, be sure to ask whether the car has seat belts before you sign the rental agreement, no matter how stupid a question it sounds.

100. How to find the latest health and safety advisories for the countries you're visiting

To find out if the countries you plan to visit have had recent political or health problems that you should be aware of, call the State Department in Washington for a continuously updated recording, at (202) 647-1488.

To find out the latest health situation for places you plan to visit, call the Centers for Disease Control Hotline in Atlanta, at (404) 639-2572.

101. How to find an English-speaking doctor when you need one

Few experiences are less welcome on vacation than trying to communicate with a health care professional in a language you don't understand well, particularly when your child needs medical help. To avoid ever needing to face that situation, contact the nonprofit International Association for Medical Assistance to Travelers (IAMAT), at 417 Center St., Lewiston, NY 14092, for membership information and for a directory of English-speaking doctors who treat IAMAT members. There is no charge for membership, although a donation is requested. The telephone number is (716) 754-4883.

You may have access to doctor referral services already, courtesy of your credit cards. American Express's Global Assist program, for example, gives you a toll-free number that you can call for referrals to English-speaking doctors in most major foreign cities and will advance you up to $5,000 to pay the bill for emergency medical services. Visa Gold cards offer traveler's assistance plans, which not only find you a doctor, but also advance you unlimited cash to pay the bill and arrange your trip home if needed. Call the service numbers for all your cards to make sure you know what's available to you.

If these methods fail you, you can always call the American embassy, which will have a list of competent physicians in various specialties who can speak your language. You can get the embassy's local number before you leave, by calling the State Department in Washington at (202) 647-5225.

Notes

Notes

Notes

Notes